THREE WORLDS

A Journey to Freedom

CUBA Y SUS JUECES COLLECTION

EDICIONES UNIVERSAL, Miami, Florida, 2021

ANTONIO GARCÍA CREWS

10/1/21
Wesley to
Very happy to
share with you
my story
Hope you enjoy it
Abuelo.

THREE WORLDS

A Journey to Freedom

--EDICIONES UNIVERSAL

First edition, 2021

EDICIONES UNIVERSAL
P.O. Box 450353 (Shenandoah Station)
Miami, FL 33245-0353. USA
(Since 1965)

E-mail: ediciones@ediciones.com
http://www.ediciones.com

Library of Congress Catalog Card No.: 2021944453
ISBN: 978-1-59388-325-6

Text preparation: María Cristina Zarraluqui

Cover design: Luis García Fresquet

This book is dedicated to

My parents
Carmen Crews (+1997) and Antonio García Cervantes (+1974)
who stayed by my side during the worst moments of my life

My wife
María Elena (Muxo) García
without her help, I would not have finished this book

Our sons and their spouses
Ignacio García y Kristin (Tritschler) García
David García y Magaly (Clavijo) García

Our grand-children
Jake, Tyler, Wesley, Lucienne and Matías

and

My companions in prison and struggles
because they also dreamed of freedom

TABLE OF CONTENTS

THREE WORLDS
A Journey to Freedom

Save us Savior of the World,
for by your Cross and Resurrection
You have set us free.

Mystery of Faith
(Order of the Mass)

ACKNOWLEDGEMENTS

I would be remiss without a special mention of those who contributed to this book by their inspiration and hard work.

María Elena, my dedicated wife and assistant in life.

Juanita Cadet, my patient and trustworthy legal assistant

Juan Manuel Salvat, my friend and publisher of this book.

Javier Figueroa, Historian.

Sixto García, Theologian, Professor and a good friend.

Basil Pflumm, my friend and role model.

Dave Wahlert, a friend since my teenage years.

Annunciation Catholic Church, my parish for almost 30 years.

PREFACE

When I finished writing these personal reflections throughout the year 2020, some other important events happened in this country where I live with my family.

The first –and very positive– was Joe Biden's victory in the November 3, 2020 elections. He was sworn in as President of the United States on January 20, 2021. In the interim between election and swearing in, during the traditional ceremony of certification of results on January 6, 2021, insurrectionists invaded the Capitol. This was a direct attack to democracy in the United States, never seen since the Civil War.

Evidently, my reflections were written while the Covit 19 pandemic overwhelmed our world.

My life developed in three very different worlds. By this I mean new situations that radically changed my life; non-chosen circumstances that left an indelible mark on me.

My first world started with birth on June 22, 1939 and extends until the Cuban State Security captured me while trying to join the fight against Fidel Castro's regime in the *Escambray* mountains in *Las Villas* province. After the arrest I was taken to death row with other men about to be executed by firing squads. However, it was decided I would undergo trial with another 30 men and be condemned to 30 years in prison. Afterwards, I was transferred to a prison in the Ile of Pines south of Havana.

My second world was spent inside several prisons. In November 1974, I enjoyed the grace of being allowed to marry María Elena, my wife of 46 years; finally left prison under parole in 1976; and the birth of our two sons. This second world ends in August 1979 upon our departure from Cuba.

The third world starts with our arrival in the United States, up to the present time. Now I have a family that makes me joyful and proud, made bigger now with two daughters-in-law and five grandchildren. My wife and I live in Orlando, Florida. I still practice immigration law since 1992 to date.

FIRST WORLD

"Traveler, the path to take has not been set yet
a path will be opened as you walk
and when you turn around to look back
you will see the path you will never again walk by".
Antonio Machado (1875-1939)

It was almost nightfall on February 5, 1961. We were traveling on a Cuban Air Force aircraft with 30 political prisoners aboard, all recently condemned, bound for the Isle of Pines. On board there was an armed militiaman and two pilots, both Air Force officers. We landed at the airport on the island –in fact rather a large key– south of the Province of Havana. There, the Model Penitentiary had been built during the Machado dictatorship in the 1930s to house political prisoners fighting against dictatorships.

From the airport we were taken by bus to the prison located a short distance away. We were met by a group of about 30 soldiers, all wielding machetes. We were issued yellow uniforms; the same as those used by former soldiers of Batista's dictatorial regime. I was bothered at having to wear the same uniform they had worn, but I had no alternative.

After putting our uniforms on we were mustered together. Amongst us was one Lieutenant of the Rebel Army who had kept his revolutionary uniform along and his star indicating his rank within Castro's army. The reaction was not long in coming. They shouted at him: "We are going to beat you up until you see stars." And so they took him away to an unknown destination. They also removed a young black man from the group. They shouted at him: "You were a monkey and the Revolution brought you down from the trees, and despite this you conspired against it. Now you will see what is going to happen to you." Those Castro soldiers were beasts.

The rest of us were taken to the Fourth Circular Building of the Model Penitentiary. While the gates were being opened I stood looking in through the iron bars. The interior of the round building was half-lit. In the middle of the circle there was a watchtower surrounded by an outside catwalk with a railing for the guard to keep watch.

I felt paralyzed at the situation facing me. Through half-shadows I saw several men in their underwear walking around the various floors. They appeared to be floating on air. They were inmates. It was akin to taking a look at a sinister place, a horror film. The gates opened and I walked in together with the rest of my group. My first life had ended, my first world, and my second one was beginning: a suffering phase that was to last until September 8, 1976.

THE BEGINNING: MY FIRST WORLD

My entry into this first world took place on June 22, 1939 at the Católicas Cubanas Clinic located in Calzada del Cerro Street in Havana, Cuba. This was two months prior to the start of World War II when Germany invaded Poland (September 1939). I was two months old at that point.

My father was a Spanish immigrant born in the Port of Cartagena, in the southwest part of Spain, facing the Mediterranean, near the Straits of Gibraltar. He had arrived in Cuba at the age of nine in 1911. He was the eldest of seven siblings, of which six were girls.

My mother was born in Cuba, daughter to an American immigrant man and a woman from Matanzas. Her name was Carmen and he married my father when they were both 34. She had studied with the nuns of the Sacred Heart in Havana and, once upon a time in her youth, had entered the convent intending on becoming a nun. The novitiate was in Albany, in the northern part of the State of New York, but she was unable to withstand the cold weather and the depression that came with it. Upon returning to Cuba she registered at the School of Science at the

University of Havana where, after graduation, she was to become a professor.

My father also went to school at the University of Havana while he worked, graduating as a Public Accountant. Since he was good at business that is what he ended up doing.

The first home of the family after my birth was a room at the Hotel Providencia on Carlos III Street in Havana. Later on my father was able to build a small house in Marianao, with the help of my godfather, who was a contractor, and so we moved there when I was one. I knew him as Uncle Emilio, a very kind man who loved us very much. The house was three blocks away from Belén School, which was to mark my life for many years to come. I refer to it as the Belén neighborhood.

Around that time General Batista was governing the country. Since my house was not far from his general headquarters, called Camp Columbia, the largest military outpost in Cuba, many in the military lived in my neighborhood. This was to be the backdrop for many important events as I was growing up.

MY FIRST SCHOOL

My first steps into the unknown world would be at the Phillips School Kindergarten, a small bilingual school where I was taught in English in the morning and in Spanish in the afternoon. Given his experience in the world of business my father wanted me to learn English. I recall that my first few days were difficult for me on account of being away from home. But little by little I got to like it and I began to have my first little friends.

I was also starting to make friends in the neighborhood. My parents hired Teresa –who I lovingly called Chacha– to look after me and to take me out to play. She would take me to many places. Every day I would play ball with the neighborhood kids. As soon as I grew up a bit I became a fan of the Almendares Baseball Club, one of four professional teams in the Havana area. The sea-son used to start in September, lasting until April, the exact opposite of the Big Leagues in the U.S. because many good Cuban players played in both places. I ended up being a New York Yankee fan too.

FIRST SHADOWS: ORFILA

In September 1947, the school year had just begun when an important event took place two blocks away from my house, in an area known as Orfila. The school bus picked me up at 2 P.M. and a little while later heavy gunfight erupted near the home of a city police officer named Morín Dopico.

The shootout lasted three or four hours, and only ended with the arrival of several tanks and regular Cuban army troops stationed in the famous general barracks of Columbia, located approximately two miles from Orfila, the scene of the battle.

My father asked members of our family who lived in the Vedado area –far from Orfila– to take me from school to their house. It was still not clear what was going on. A while later my parents learned that there were rivalries between two gangs within the police department itself.

THE SUMMER

My family life was kept away from all the political issues of the day. The school year ended and three months of vacation were approaching. Taking into account that I had already learned enough English, my parents decided it was time for me to enjoy summer camp in the U.S. in order to improve it. In 1947, at the early age of eight, I was off to Dixie Camp near Atlanta, and the following three consecutive years to Camp Acadia in Upstate New York.

At Camp Acadia (north of New York City), I could communicate well in English, and also improve it, since I had already learned a lot in grammar school. I am very thankful to my father for having the good idea of getting me started early in the English language.

My stay at the camp for three summers in a row –and being able to get to know New York– opened my imagination a lot. At camp I stood out as a good baseball player and I learned to play basketball, which soon became my favorite sport. Having just turned nine during my first year at the camp, I was runner up to the Best Camper Award. The following year I was captain of a team and again runner up to the Best Athlete Award in the Juniors Division. The third summer was a disaster, I ended up sick with pneumonia, but I remember giving a girl my first kiss.

BELÉN SCHOOL, MARIANAO, CUBA

In 1949, my hoped-for dream of entering Belén School became a reality. I started there in the 4th grade. It was the best experience of my life up to that moment. Prior to this time, from the corner of my house, I would watch the school's buses laden with children. At that time Belén had an impressive structure, looking more like a university. More than 1,000 students were enrolled there.

In a certain way one stage of my life –Phillips School– was left behind. I kept in touch with my good friends from the neighborhood, who even up to this day are still my good friends. Belén was another world. Just in the 4th grade there were four sections of 25 students each –almost 100 students. I recall that the religious in charge of the 5th Division (where the 4th grade resided) was called Brother Gonzalito. He loved to play soccer with us –which was the favorite sport among Spanish priests. Almost all Jesuit priests in Belén were Spaniards. The school curriculum in Belén was more difficult and disciplined that at the Phillips School, but English class was below level for me. Therefore, that first year my single academic award was in English class.

Fifth grade went very well for me, but I did not end up in the top four of my class because the teacher would force me to write with my right hand whereas I am left handed. My penmanship was awful. It was a big trauma for me to lose the prize for this reason. My father was irate about this injustice. However, I had begun to feel a sense of endearment for my school.

The following school year was called "Pre-High School"– I did well, among the first four in the class. Finally, they respected my being left handed and just let it be. Since I lived very near the school, I could stay to play in the school fields. The school day began at Belén with a Mass and ended with the Rosary. I felt happy in school.

= ○ = ○ = ○ =

A NOTE ABOUT THE POLITICAL SITUATION

My father was an innate businessman. During those times he was a partner at a company called Víveres, S.A. They were importers and distributors of Oliveite, the leading cooking oil brand in Cuba. Therefore, we had everything we could ever want at home. At that time Carlos Prío Socarrás governed Cuba as part of the Partido Auténtico (Authentic Party). His term was to go from 1948 to 1952. He was to be the second president elected through democratic elections in Cuba. His term was to end in June 1952. My father was not much interested in politics, but I recall he voted for Prío. His term didn't end well because General Batista, the former dictator, headed a coup d'état on March 10, 1952.

MY BACKGROUND AND FAMILY HISTORY

Now in my first year in high school I joined the school's basketball team. I was also a member of the Habana Yacht Club. This was on account of my maternal grandfather, Thomas D. Crews, as I noted before, an American immigrant who met my grandmother, Sofía Carrerá, a girl from Matanzas, in Jacksonville, Florida. She was in Jacksonville because her uncle, medical doctor José Angulo, a freedom fighter against Spain had had to seek refuge in the U.S. together with his family. Later they met again after the War of Independence, known in the U.S. as the Spanish-American War of 1898. My grandfather was sent to Cuba as part of the U.S. Army. They married and had three children: Joseph, Mercy, and Carmen (my mom). They were a close family. One of their traditions was to celebrate Thanksgiving Day on the 4th Thursday of November. We would meet at my grandparents' house. As this is a U.S. custom it was not celebrated in Cuba.

Around that time I studied Ancient and Middle Age History as part of the high school curriculum, discovering something up to then unknown to me: my vocation for History. The following year it was my turn to study Modern and Contemporary History, something that was to strengthen my vocation even more.

World War II had ended in 1945 but the effects of the Cold War were ever more present. I recall perfectly well a newsreel by Metro Goldwin Mayer which was shown weekly in the movie theaters before the film. The Soviet Communists had been able to test an atomic bomb and a hydrogen one too. It seemed that the world was headed to World War III, this time a nuclear war which would put an end to humanity as we knew it. This was something that was etched in my mind.

On the other hand I was getting into my adolescent years. At the Yacht Club I was part of a large group of friends, and I was getting invited to many parties. The influence of American pop music was big amongst us all. Havana was –to a certain extent– like any U.S. city if you take into account the technological advances we enjoyed: late-model automobiles, TV sets, etc. However, our history and culture was very different from that of the U.S.... and we proudly spoke Spanish. This was Havana, and the rest of the cities in Cuba we used to call the countryside with an air of superiority.

Beliefs and Spirituality

Evidently my religious beliefs I owe to the Catholic Church. I am Catholic by birth. I was baptized at the Church of El Carmen in Havana in August 1939. My First Communion I took at the age of seven, and my Confirmation at Belén School. Yet my spirituality was bred by my mother. I remember how she would lead me to pray at home, next to my first bed, an image of the Sacred Heart of Jesus hanging from the wall in front of me. My baptismal name is Antonio Paulino del Corazón de Jesús. I consider her to be the foundation of my Christian spirituality. My mother insisted a lot with my father that I be registered to go to Belén School, although my father was opposed to the idea. He wanted me to continue to study at Phillips and improve my English.

Political Unrest: the Coup d'état

On March 10, 1952, General Batista undertook a coup, 90 days before the scheduled elections to be held June 1, 1952. In 1933, Batista had been a sergeant in the Cuban Army. That year there was a rebellion against the dictatorship of General Machado (his regime was known as El Machadato). In 1934, Batista became Chief of the Army and of the Government, a strong man controlling presidents until 1940, when he became President of Cuba through elections.

Batista's presidency ended in 1944, when, afraid for his life he left Cuba for Daytona Beach, Florida.

In 1944, medical doctor Ramón Grau San Martín –former revolutionary in 1933, and a member of the Partido Auténtico– was elected President in clean elections.

In 1948, he was succeeded in power by a member of his own party, Carlos Prío Socarrás, this time also in clean elections, but there is no doubt that in the administrations of these two Authentic Party members there was corruption. When Batista conducted the coup d'état in 1952, his argument for it was "ending corruption."

I clearly recall the coup on March 10th on television. Batista appeared from Camp Columbia, two miles away from my home. That afternoon I saw some of my neighbors crying because what had happened.

My father, as a businessman, I don't think knew much about politics in Cuba. However, he sympathized with Batista at first because he was going to put things in order and end the corruption.

I was 13 at the time doing my Pre-High School year. In school everything went on as usual. But, from this moment on, my life would begin to change slowly but radically.

My Trip to Europe

In 1954, having just turned 15 years of age, my father invited us –my mother, my cousin Eddy and me– to a unique experience, something which none of my schoolmates had lived: a trip to Europe.

In June we left from New York aboard the *Andrea Doria,* an Italian ship considered classy. We sailed for eight days. We crossed the Atlantic, passed by Gibraltar and entered the Mediterranean to disembark in Naples. From there we visited Pompey skirting the Amalfi coast into the island of Capri. My small world had opened up considerably. I was fascinated. The four of us were on a Fiat car that my father had rented, with an Italian driver named Sacco who knew Italy to the hilt.

Then we went to Rome, which impacted me greatly because it was a city that weaves three histories: the history of Rome as a city, the history of Christianity and the history of the Italian Republic. Given my interest in history, Rome quickly became my preferred city: The Colisseum, the Roman Forum, Saint Peter's, Saint Paul Outside the Walls, Saint Mary Major, Saint John Lateran, all are part of the marvelous history of Christendom.

At Saint Peter's we participated in a Mass officiated by Pius XII. It was emotional. At the entrance to Saint Peter's, in front of us, was a large group of American sailors. When the Pope made his entrance they hailed him throwing their caps to the air. We also visited the monument to Victor Emmanuel II, the first king to unite Italy as a country. It was in Rome where I realized the universality of my Christian faith.

My mom wanted to see Assisi, the land of Saint Francis, while my father wanted to visit Padua because of Saint Anthony, his patron saint. Then, continuing through the North we visited the great lakes: Maggiore and Cuomo, crossing over the San Gottardo Pass into Switzerland. On the mountain peaks I saw snow for the first time in my life –although we were in summer. We went on to Lucerne and Geneva. The country seemed beautiful to me.

In France we visited several cities. In Paris my mom was dying to take us to the *Sacré Coeur* (Sacred Heart church), with a panoramic view of the whole city. I had finished my second year of high school and I had already studied the French Revolution and Napoleon's exploits, so therefore I enjoyed the city greatly.

We went on to Spain, entering through *San Sebastián*. We spent a week there, relaxing and dancing. I was impressed by the Spanish women. Then, in Madrid, there was much to see, but the most impressive sight for me was El Escorial, Phillip II's palace. When we were there, Franco was building the Valley of the Fallen in the location where José Antonio Primo de Rivera, founder of the Falangist Movement, was buried. Franco himself would later be buried there too.

After Madrid, we went south to Córdoba, Seville and Granada, where we saw a bull fight. Finally we got to Cartagena my father's home town. There, we found some of his mother's relatives, the Cervantes. My father threw a street party which we all enjoyed. Upon arriving in Barcelona we bid good-bye to Sacco, our Italian guide.

We returned to Cuba on KLM with stops in Amsterdam and Montreal before landing in Havana. It was October 1954.

= o = o = o =

Now back in Cuba, my sole interest turned to sports, parties and girls. I was just trying to pass my grade and do my homework with the least possible effort. I had already taken up the practice of basketball, baseball and track and field (especially the javelin). This took up a lot of time and effort. My junior year of high school was disastrous. Only the History of Cuba, Psychology and Civics held an interest for me, given my strong social vocation.

The Ethics & Civics class I was studying the political structure of our nation, based on Cuba's 1940 Constitution. Our teacher was José Ignacio Rasco, a former student leader at the University of Havana who had graduated first of his Belen class in 1945, then went on to study Law. He had a charismatic personality which spirited the class. He organized a Parliament among the students calling for elections for the positions of Head of the Assembly and Secretary. I ran for Head of the Assembly and lost, but I was designated Secretary of the Assembly. I felt motivated by politics for the first time in my life, in a country that was suffering under the Batista dictatorship. This class made me think about new horizons.

I was not much concerned with what was going on around the world. My interpretation was simple: the world was divided into two big sides, one good and one bad —the good side was led by the U.S. and the bad by Soviet Communists. Cuba was aligned with the good guys. I lived in Havana where we had television, model-year cars and the latest novelties, just like in the U.S.

At school our team had won the basketball championship (for under 15) in 1954. We had gone to play in Santiago de Cuba against the Dolores Jesuit School. It was a great experience to visit Santiago for the first time and I was able to visit the Basilica of El Cobre, in honor of Cuba's patroness, who appeared to three fishermen in the year 1612.

September 1956: Beginning of Conciousness

My senior year in high school came with a surprise. We got a visit from Humberto Alvira, a member of the University Catholic Group (Agrupación Católica Universitaria, ACU) to make a presentation to us about the Social Doctrine of the Catholic Church. The topic was fairly new to us. Alvira was a great activist and he encouraged us to create a social group for the study of the Doctrine. We began to meet after the mandatory daily mass at school.

Belén also assigned a "Maestrillo" to the seniors – which were Jesuits on their way to be ordained. His name was Father Camacho, and he also encouraged us to join the study group on the Doctrine, in which he would also take part. The project was going well –the meetings were held on Sundays and Humberto Alvira was the lecturer during conferences about the Dignity of the Human Person, Social Justice, the Common Good, the Family, etc. We also studied the most important Papal encyclicals of the day: *Rerum Novarum, Quadragessimo Anno* and the Christmas homilies by Pope Pius XII. There was lots of excitement; all my close friends took part. From this group the idea was born to visit the "Corea de La Lisa", an extremely poor slum in the outskirts of Marianao, near the cemetery. Only a few nuns were offering material and spiritual aid there. When we visited the place they told us about a family in particular who needed more help than the others.

The group of us decided to spend our Christmas vacation working there every day. We laid down a cement floor as they were living on a pounded dirt floor. We built a latrine (they lacked a bathroom) and we brought them a Christmas meal to share with them. It was a very poor neighborhood where many needs went unattended. To me this experience was a great discovery. It enlightened by conscience. After work, in the evenings, I never missed one of the Christmas parties with my friends from the Habana Yacht Club. This placed me face to face with a big contradiction which made me think: on the one hand was my life of privilege, which up to that time I had not realized, where I lacked nothing. On the other hand, was the life of the poor in the neighborhood of Corea. The gap was abysmal. One night in particular, while I was enjoying myself with my friend Manolo Comellas (Cawy) at the home of a very rich family, the party ended as we were watering the lawn with champagne. On my way home that night I thought long and hard about this dysfunctional disparity. Christ awoke my conscience.

After the Christmas experience, an even bigger plan was hatched for "La Corea". We had a Biology teacher named Lino Fernández, a physician and member of the ACU. We invited him to come with us and he suggested we create a medical dispensary like others he knew about within the ACU's program to create such centers in underprivileged neighborhoods in Havana. We thought it was a great idea. Our Social Doctrine group spread the news among the students of the 1957 class and many decided to also take part in its construction.

= o = o = o =

On November 30, 1956 a very important event happened: Fidel Castro landed in *Oriente* province. I didn't know who Castro was and I found out that he had been jailed for his attack to the Moncada barracks in *Oriente,* in 1953.

On March, 13, 1957 the Presidential Palace in Havana was attacked in search of the president Fulgencio Batista. I was at school during recess at 3 P.M. with Eddie Blanco, a classmate. We gathered around a car radio to listen to the breaking news from Radio Reloj.

At that very moment there was an interruption and we heard the voice of José Antonio Echeverría, President of the Student Federation of the University of Havana (FEU) saying that the President had been killed inside the Palace. My classmate and I ran to spread the news to senior class in school. We stood at the main entrance of the school and were able to see army tanks going down Columbia Avenue bound for the Presidential Palace. This was the first political event I witnessed and it meant for me that a new road was being shaped in Cuba.

José Antonio Echeverría died a few minutes later in a shootout next to the university where he had tried to hide after his takeover of the radio station. Belén students declared a class strike day in solidarity with José Antonio Echeverría. These developments were for us a sign that something new was afoot.

= ∘ = ∘ = ∘ =

Meanwhile, the school year continued, in spite of the events.

During this, my last high school year, I participated in what was called the Avellaneda Literary Academy, where we learned the art of speaking in public. In remembrance of the death of José Martí on May 19th, the Academy organized an event which we called "Belén Graduates Face the Future of Cuba." It was presided over by Father Daniel Baldor, SJ, the Cuban priest who sponsored our course. Father Rafael Camacho was also present. Several topics were presented regarding Cuban issues: politics, the economy, religion, etc. I was assigned to speak on Education and Morality. We were very excited with great ideas to reform the Republic which was suffering from a dictatorship and a lot of political and financial corruption. There was also a big problem of social injustice towards wide segments of the poor population, something we had gotten to know well at "Corea de la Lisa".

The student President of the Avellaneda Academy was Domingo Domínguez Lamoglia. Domingo had had his arm amputated because of cancer. He was selected to say the valedictorian speech on the evening of our graduation a few days later, on June 14, 1957. His speech was extraordinary –I will never forget it. He finished by saying "To become heroes or simply failures solely depends on us." Today, at age 80, and after a long life's path I would say: "It only depends on Christ's action in our lives when we open up our hearts to him."

I did not achieve any academic awards at my graduation, but they did give me the recognition of being the Best Athlete in the 1957 school year.

Before our graduation from Belén, we discovered the yearbook *"Ecos"* on the occasion of the 1945 graduation where several known personalities appeared: one such was José Ignacio Rasco who had exerted a great influence over the 1957 graduates as Civics teacher and later on when he became a professor and lawyer. Fidel Castro was shown. At the time, he was leading the guerillas against Batista. He had played basketball and baseball, earning the prize as Best Athlete of his year. He had also participated in the Avellaneda Literary Academy in his time. In the yearbook's photo captions of the graduating students, under his photo it read: "Fidel will write important pages in the history of this nation. He has what it takes".

This made me think a lot. I was a young man, politically illiterate as I was leaving Belén, but I cherished deep values and a great love for Christ and his mother Mary. I aimed for a political and constitutional democracy, abused as it had been by Fulgencio Batista. Now I had added a yearning for social justice after having studied it more thoroughly and having gone through the experience in the slums.

My Father and His Plans for Me

My father wanted me to study Accounting, but I didn't like it and I was more inclined for Economics which, I believed, had a strong social content. I registered at the University of Villanueva, headed by Augustinian priests, on the outskirts of Marianao. Classes were to start in September 1957. But my father wanted me to spend a summer working in Dubuque, Iowa, at the meat packing company of Bob Wahlert, his provider of hams and other products, whom he personally knew and respected. I lived an experience which was very different from what my life had been up to then. I was lodged at the YMCA in Dubuque while working during the day in July

– also met Mr. Wahlert's four children. One of them was a contemporary of mine, an "adventure" buddy. All treated me very well while showing an interest over what was going on in Cuba. I talked to them about my favorable views of Castro and his guerillas. *Time* magazine had published an interview with Fidel Castro while in the *Sierra Maestra*, written by Herbert Matthews, a famous journalist of *The New York Times.* In Dubuque I learned a lot about the meat packing business that my father considered important for me as he was just then beginning the construction of a meat packing facility in Santa María del Rosario, just outside the city of Havana.

I returned to Havana aboard a ferry from West Palm Beach with two young friends: Bob Wahlert Jr. and Richard Weber. The rest of the summer was spent in Varadero beach in my father's recently purchased apartment.

= o = o = o =

My Life and College Activities

The new school year began in September when I started my first year in the School of Economic Sciences. To obtain a Bachelor's Degree required three years of coursework and I was motivated to do battle for social justice in Cuba.

I also started visiting the Agrupación Católica Universitaria (ACU), a Marian congregation where Humberto Alvira was Head of Apostolate. The congregation had been founded in the 1930s by the Spanish Jesuit priest Felipe Rey de Castro. In 1957 the Father Director was Armando Llorente.

I was encouraged by a research study about Cuban agricultural workers that ACU had undertaken. This type of worker would cut sugarcane, the main source of wealth in Cuba. However, most of these workers lived in abject poverty (their daily salary was on average $0.25) especially outside the months of the sugar harvest.

My life was changing quickly and radically. The ACU's building was next to the University of Havana –at the corner of

Mazón and San Miguel– very far from my house, which my father had built recently in a new neighborhood in Marianao, called Country Club, very near the University of Villanueva, the Habana Yacht Club, and the Corpus Christi Church; but far from the ACU site. In order to make possible my travels and activities, he gave me a model-year Studebaker car at the end of the summer.

The ACU was very attractive because it was a gathering place for students from three universities in Havana. It was a corner building and had enough space for boarding students from outside the capital. I was admitted to join the group of candidates directed by a member in charge of training. We would attend classes every week during the span of one year. We also participated in a Church Social Doctrine session conducted by Humberto Alvira, whom I had known since my fifth year of high school at Belén School.

I was chosen Assistant Director of a small school in the *"Corea de la Lisa"* neighborhood, charged with teaching very basic English to children I knew well. I was able to do this thanks to what I learned at the Phillips School up to 3rd grade and because of time spent in the U.S.

With me were several classmates who graduated together from Belén and had joined ACU: Julián Martínez, Manolo Hidalgo, Joaquín Pérez, Ricardo Puerta, Eduardo Muñiz and Rolando Castañeda. Our enthusiasm knew no limit, we wanted to change Cuba and to make it better. The political situation in Cuba was getting worse and Fidel Castro's movement (named 26 of July) was growing in Havana and other cities. Fidel Castro was still up in the Sierra Maestra mountains.

At times, anti-Batista activists planted bombs to explode in the middle of the night in places where people gathered in order to terrify the population. The year 1958 was one of turmoil from the start. There was talk of a call to a general strike on April 9th to take down the dictatorship. Since the university had already shut down, students from Villanueva organized –for the first time– a

33

student association. I was elected to represent the School of Economics. We met and agreed to support the general strike and to close our university as well.

The strike was a failure, but all this did not frighten my father who demanded that I go to work with him to his business warehouse where a train brought the oil, lard and other food items. The goods were coming via ferry from West Palm Beach, arriving at the Port of Havana to be distributed by train to the city. The owner of the ferry company was a millionaire from West Palm Beach who also owned the famous Breakers Hotel.

In June 1958, the University of Villanueva restarted classes. We were able to finish the school year during the summer and start second year in October. At the ACU I was told of my promotion to full membership at the Vigil of the Immaculate Conception (December 7th). Among the selected were my beloved friends of so many years: Manuel Hidalgo, Ricardo Puerta, Manuel Salvat, Luis Fernandez Rocha, Julián Martínez Inclán, and Carlos Rodríguez Santana. I still have the medal of the Immaculate Conception with my name engraved on it, given to me on that day. It kept me company while I was in prison.

There was a political group among the members which a few days before I had decided to join in the struggle against Batista: the Legion of Revolutionary Action (Legión de Acción Revolucionaria, LAR. Batista organized an electoral farce while denying the opposition any political liberty. Andrés Rivero Agüero, an unknown follower of Batista, was "elected".

I continued my work at the ACU to the point that it became my second home. Relaxing in its backyard, under the shade of almond trees, the members would chat – students and professors. I recall a conversation I had with a medical student, Javier Calvo, with whom I established a good friendship. He was the one who introduced me to the theology of Romano Guardini, thus far unknown to me. Cardinal Guardini exerts great influence on Pope Francis ideals even today.

Mid-December 1958 I learned that Father Armando Llorente, SJ, the Director of ACU, had traveled to the *Sierra Maestra* to visit Fidel Castro, his former student at Belén. Upon his return Llorente was very excited with the reception that Castro had extended to him. I decided to ask him for an interview as I wanted to join the insurrection in the mountains. He gave me the names of some classmates who were to go first, and he suggested I speak with Ricardo Puerta, my school friend.

Christmastime was over and on December 26th, 1958, I met with Julián Martínez Inclán at the now familiar ACU backyard. He told me that he was going to join the rebellion in the mountains of Pinar del Río (west of Havana). He asked me to drive him there in my car and to return to Havana afterwards. I didn't accept because I had another commitments and didn't find out what became of him until several days later.

On December 31, 1958 we heard rumors that Lieutenant Ventura –reputable for being the worst murderer of Batista's police in Havana– had said ACU members were conspiring against Batista. The ACU recommended to us not to return to our own homes. I mentioned it to my father who talked to a close friend of his and asked him to give me shelter at his house. I always carried a portable radio/tape recorder which I took with me there, then went to bed early. At about 4 a.m. I heard someone knocking at the door and thought the police was coming for me. I ran in my pajamas towards the backyard. The house was surrounded by a short wall and while I was trying to jump over it, I heard someone yelling: "Batista fled!". I returned to the house and turned the radio on. They were already confirming the news flash that Batista had fled Cuba. From the *Sierra Maestra* mountains, the clandestine radio news was repeating the same information. I was able to tape it all.

Fidel Castro declared: "The tyrant has left his den. From this moment on we declare a general strike in support of the Revolution – Santiago de Cuba (capital city of Oriente Province) is not yet free, but it will not be like in 1899 when the Mambises troops of General Calixto García were not allowed to enter its streets." This was in reference to a historic fact from the end of the Spanish-American War: Cuban rebel Mambises were not allowed to march in the streets of Santiago de Cuba after the Spanish troops had surrendered to the U.S.

My happiness knew no bounds. The dictatorship had become increasingly oppressive, causing many deaths, thus antagonizing the population in general. I called home to tell my parents I was coming back home. The streets were very crowded – cars honking. It was total paroxism but nobody knew what to do next.

Fidel Castro entered Santiago de Cuba and the Army offered no resistance. He named Manuel Urrutia Lleó –a judge– to become President of the Republic, ordering him to go to Havana. The guerillas lead by Ernesto "Che" Guevara and Camilo Cienfuegos got orders from Fidel Castro to advance from Las Villas to Havana to take over the military bases of La Cabaña and Columbia.

On January 3, 1959, friends called me to let me know that Julián Martínez Inclán, Javier Calvo and three others from his group had been captured, tortured and murdered by Batista's troops on December 28th in the mountains of Pinar del Río. My pain was deep. Julián was my great friend since Belén School. We used to study together, we would go to the movies and we played basketball in the same team. Everything had changed for me now. A new stage of my life started

= ○ = ○ = ○ =

The Triumphal Revolution

The first few days of the year 1959 –and of the Revolution– were a great joy due to what had happened, but at the same time, they were days of mourning and great pain for the ACU due to the assassination of four members, in addition to another victim who was a Captain of the Revolutionary Directorate. Total: five.

One day I was standing by the door of the ACU when I saw Manolo Artime, recently arrived with the troops from the Sierra Maestra. I was the first to see him and welcome him. Since I was a member of the Legion of Revolutionary Action (LAR in Spanish) I was asked and I accepted to join the group guarding the Electricity Company to avoid sabotage by Batista elements that were still prowling around the city. All in all I spent only three nights on this mission.

Soon thereafter some friends from the Belén neighborhood told me that Camilo Cienfuegos and his troops were headed to the Columbia Military Camp –the largest in Cuba. I waited at Belén's gate (6th Street) and was able to see everything. I saw more than 100 cars full of rebel soldiers go by. The old army had already surrendered and so Camilo Cienfuegos entered the camp without firing a shot.

Fidel Castro, meanwhile, was slowly making his way from Oriente, stopping at every provincial capital city to make a speech. On January 8th he entered Havana. I was at the ACU near L and 23rd Streets in front of the Hilton Hotel. In the afternoon the caravan went by in front of us, on top of a tank was Fidel Castro followed by many others. We got back to the ACU to be able to watch the rest of the route on television. And so we were able to watch and listen to the first speech by Fidel Castro in Havana, upon arriving at Camp Columbia. It was a historic event where he promised general elections in three months.

In the middle of January 1959, the revolutionary government issued a law (Act 11) to punish those of us students who had continued to go to class in private universities after the University of Havana had closed its doors. This led to a coordinated action by all private schools to protest this law. After a few days, it was annulled.

Towards the end of January 1959, I met Father Cavero, SJ at the ACU. This Spaniard had been at the *Sierra Maestra*. The priest was making plans to teach classes to Fidel Castro's soldiers (known as "the bearded ones") assigned to the military garrisons around Havana. Finally he selected the military base in *Managua*. A group of us offered to help out. I also volunteered and he named me Principal of that school. Classes started at the end of January. Our class schedule was in the afternoons daily. We had around 20 rebel soldiers as students. Basic classes were taught in reading, writing, arithmetic and catechism.

One day I was not allowed to enter. The reason was that there was a sort of troop mutiny going on and Fidel Castro was called in to talk to them and restore calm. In my case I protested to the soldier and asked to speak to the Camp Commander, Major Juan Almeida. Next to him there was a third person listening to the conversation. He turned around and said: "I am Juan Almeida." In the midst of my obfuscation I picked up my books and quickly left. The following day I was allowed to come in and I found out what the problem had been: several former officers of the Batista army had been charged with holding classes on military discipline to the "bearded ones", and these had rebelled.

Many events took place during that first month of the year: every day Fidel Castro would appear in TV to give long speeches. At this point he had not assigned himself an official post in the new administration. Firing squads were established to be used against officers and soldiers of Batista's Army accused of committing atrocities –many without a trial.

At the beginning of February 1959 the ACU invited Rebel Army Captain Jaime Goiricelalla to speak to the group. He had been a member of Raúl Castro's column at the Sierra Maestra. Word was out that there was an ongoing Communist infiltration at the top of the revolutionary hierarchy. Goiricelalla explained to us that there were Communists in Raúl Castro's group but that neither the Revolution nor Fidel Castro were Communist. He added that it was necessary to influence from within to avoid having them gain strength. At this point in time ACU member **Rogelio González Corso,** an agronomist, was also present. At the time he held an important post at the Ministry of Agriculture, under its Minister Humberto Sorí Marín, a Major in the Sierra Maestra (Comandante or Major was the highest rank in the Rebel Army).

= ∘ = ∘ = ∘ =

Rural Commandos

Since we were still waiting for classes to re-open at the universities, some ACU members decided to volunteer to teach classes in the countryside in an area near to what had been a guerilla camp at the Sierra Maestra. So we got ready for the trip to the Sierra in Oriente, at the opposite end of the island. I resigned from my teaching in Managua and at the end of February we left by train bound for Bayamo. We were about 40 members participating. When we got there Manuel Artime took us to Manzanillo by bus and the following day to the Estrada Palma Sugar Mill. From there we walked four hours to Guasimilla de Nagua.

My experience as a rural teacher at the Sierra Maestra was extraordinary. It allowed me to know how Cuban peasants really lived. They lived in thatched roof huts with dirt floors called *bohíos,* a Taíno Indian word. I lived in one of these and slept on a hammock. From this place I could see the Turquino Peak –the highest elevation in Cuba. We would eat with the family to which we had been assigned: typically two fried eggs with rice and red beans. Breakfast was coffee with milk and bread. After breakfast we would walk two to three miles through the woods to get to the school house, built with boards made from palm trees. There, I was teaching elementary school as well as reading & writing. There were 40 to 50 kids attending. The peasants were very happy with the Revolution – nobody even mentioned Communism, although I do recall there was a group of Communists who one time argued with me because I was criticizing Communism every time I got the opportunity to do so.

The peasants were coffee farmers and some were still in the process of paying for the installment plan of the land they were planting. Everyone was awaiting a promised Agrarian Reform Law that would make them owners of these lands. I was working for the Ministry of Agriculture lead by its Minister Sorí Marín.

Guasimilla was about four hours away on foot from the Estrada Palma Sugar Mill, the largest sugar mill situated in the town of Yara, in the southern part of the Oriente province. After the two scheduled months (March and April), Manuel Artime visited us and we had a big good-bye get together. We gathered around one thousand peasants coming from all the hills where the literacy corps had been working. On May 1, 1959 –in the early morning hours– we headed off on foot from Guasimilla to the Estrada Palma Sugar Mill to take part in a rally in the city of Manzanillo, together with Artime and one of the Revolution Comandantes.

During my stay at the Sierra Maestra, **Humberto Alvira**, the Head of Apostolate of the Agrupación Católica Universitaria (ACU), was killed in a traffic accident. Another good friend, Ernesto Fernández Travieso, was hurt. They were on their way to visit the Literacy Corps in Oriente. Upon my return to the ACU in Havana I was named Head of Apostolate replacing Humberto. I decide then to resign from membership of the League of Revolutionary Action (LAR) as I didn't want to mix a political commitment with my pastoral and apostolic work.

The University of Havana

On May 11 1959, the University of Havana reopened its doors. I participated in the opening student rally. I had registered in the School of Social Sciences and remember that day well. All the top leaders of the Revolution were in attendance: Fidel Castro –who had now elevated himself to Prime Minister, the President of the

Republic Manuel Urrutia, and Comandantes Ernesto "Che" Guevara and Faure Chomón. All had the opportunity to speak to the college students.

In June 1959 the University of Villanueva also reopened. I remember that I had to go to summer classes in order to finish off my second year in Economics. In the new academic year starting in September 1959 I began my 3rd year in Economics and 1st year in Social Sciences in both universities. It was challenging for me, but my energy and enthusiasm knew no bounds.

$$= \circ = \circ = \circ =$$

June 1959 was a sadly memorable month. Fidel Castro forced President Urrutia to resign his post after the latter had denounced that the Revolution was infiltrated by Communist elements. Towards the end of October, Húber Matos, "Comandante de la Revolución" in charge of Camagüey province wrote a letter denouncing the infiltration of the Revolution by Communist elements as well. This caused him to be arrested and sentenced to 20 years in prison so the political situation was becoming increasingly grave and dangerous.

In October 1959, Cuba's National Labor Union (Central de Trabajadores de Cuba, CTC) organized an important Congress. Two of its member: Reinol González and José de Jesús Planas –both coming out of the Young Catholic Workers (Juventud Obrera Católica, JOC) – were at the time Secretary of Public Relations and Legal Secretary of the CTC, respectively. Through them I was able to bring to the CTC a box full of 1000 pamphlets that showed the connection of the Communist Party with Batista in the early 1940s. It was entitled: *Batista Father of Communism.* Its author was a Jesuit priest and it had been published by Oscar Echeverría in his print shop. We were able to distribute the brochures which were used to mobilize anti-Communist leaders inside the CTC. A joke at the time described the Revolution as a watermelon: green on the outside (as the Rebel Army wore olive green uniforms) and red the inside (for the worldwide Communist movement). The simile stuck and it spread widely. Reinol and Planas were demoted from the CTC leadership, as well as David Salvador, its President.

My activities didn't cease. In December 1959 I traveled to Chile with Luis Fernández-Rocha – representing the ACU and the School of Medicine– to attend the Youth Conference. There I had the opportunity to meet then Senator Eduardo Frei, President of Chile's Christian Democratic Party, as well as other party members.

$$= \circ = \circ = \circ =$$

The Approaching Storm

The year 1959 was ending and one could already feel stormy winds blowing. Fidel Castro totally controlled the political situation in Cuba. On January 8, 1959 he had stated that he would call for general elections in three months; later he prolonged it to six months and finally he publicly launched the slogan: "Elections, what for?" The campaign to eliminate elections had started.

In early 1960 we were told that Anastas Mikoyan, the then Minister of Commerce of the Soviet Union, had been invited to visit Cuba to inaugurate a Soviet Exhibit in February. The Soviets had been involved in the Invasion of Hungary in October 1956. The members of the ACU conceived the idea to organize a demonstration (mostly made up of students) at the University of Havana against Mikoyan's visit to Cuba. We met several times to discuss our options. I decided to visit Mateo Jover, President of Cuba's Catholic Action (Acción Católica) to conduct a joint action during his visit. Catholics perceived the Soviet Union as an enemy on account of being totalitarian, atheist and an enemy of the Church. Jover declined to join.

The ACU ended up deciding to hold an event at Havana's Central Park on February 5, 1960 after the traditional wreath offering in front of the statue of José Martí by Mikoyan. We prepared signs with slogans like: Hail the Revolution –Down with Communism, Hail Fidel –Down with Mikoyan, Free Elections, and so on. We used our personal contacts to invite a good number of people.

Mikoyan deposited his wreath in the morning accompanied by Fidel Castro. After the ceremony they moved on to the Museum of Fine Arts (Museo de Bellas Artes) to inaugurate the exhibit. At 11:30 a.m. I left the ACU in my car with another four colleagues headed to Central Park. Our event had been called for at noon. Already close to the place, at Prado and Colón Streets the police stopped us because one of the occupants in the car was flying leaflets directing people to go to the park. The Police agent ordered me to drive to the closest Police Station where he opened the trunk where the signs were. He ushered us into the Station. Soon a shooting was heard nearby. It was done by the authorities –not by the demonstrators. New prisoners joined us. Some of them we knew, including a woman, Julita Díaz. They had in fact been at the Central Park and so we were able to find out about what had happened. Still others escaped to safety. In front of the Police Station a few hundred people showed up shouting: "To the firing squads!". It was the slogan used to frighten "counter-revolutionaries". Then we were sent in patrol cars to the Castillo de La Punta, a historic fort turned into a detention center. We were 21 students in all who spent the night in jail. Efigenio Almejeiras, the city Chief of Police, addressed us the following day at noon advising us to not allow ourselves to be "manipulated by the Imperialism". Then, he set us free.

$$= \circ = \circ = \circ =$$

I stop now to analyze the situation at this point in time. I was 19 years old and still had a few months left to graduate in Economics from the University of Villanueva. I was already convinced that the so-called revolution that had "freed" the country was itself a dictatorship headed in the direction of implementing a dictatorship, worse than the previous one: a Communist dictatorship that would guarantee Fidel Castro the absolute and permanent power he yearned for. This was only the beginning. In our case, there was no explanation to jail a group of peaceful and unarmed demonstrators.

In March 1960, the Students Federation –Federación Estudiantil Universitaria (FEU)– through its President, Comandante Rolando Cubelas, called for a student meeting where he stated that the FEU's position was: "no capitalism or communism". It ended peacefully. A few days later, due to pressures from the university communists, Cubelas called for another meeting where he accused the Central Park rally participants of working against the Revolution and, therefore, subject to punishment. Alberto Muller, Juan Manuel Salvat and Ernesto Fernandez Travieso were expelled from the university; Joaquin Pérez was beaten by pro-regime students. Due to these threats I decided to stay away from the University of Havana and focus in finishing my degree at the University of Villanueva. Already some ACU members had decided to leave the country with the goal of joining a camp in Guatemala directed by the U.S. Among them was Carlos Rodríguez Santana, a childhood friend from the Mariano neighborhood.

After a while hiding in my house, Salvat was able to get asylum in an embassy in Havana together with Alberto Muller and Ernesto Fernández Travieso, and all eventually were able to travel to the U.S. At his time it was already possible to listen to the short-wave radio broadcast of Radio Swan from abroad with content that was not allowed in Cuba. In my opinion these news were not trustworthy and I held the opinion that the struggle against Castro had to take place inside Cuba, where Fidel Castro still enjoyed wide popularity.

At the time my father was encouraging me to seek admission in a U.S. university to obtain a Master's Degree right after graduation from Villanueva. Sometime later I realized that my father was desperately trying to avoid the kind of future that awaited me.

44

Northward Bound

In July 1960, I graduated from the University of Villanueva with a Bachelor's Degree in Economics. The University of Chicago admitted me to study a Master's Degree in that discipline. My father asked a friend and business associate, Robert Wahlert (previously mentioned in this diary), President of the Dubuque Packing Company, to lodge me at his home until the beginning of the college year in September. He agreed –something I considered a great honor– and so at the end of the month I flew from Havana to Chicago. There I stayed at the Palmer Hotel where I visited another business partner of my father's in Cuba, Alvin Kline. I recall that he went with me to buy a suit and a heavy winter coat. Later I departed for Dubuque aboard Bob Wahlert, Jr.'s private plane, who had become my friend during my first visit in 1957.

Dubuque was a small town of 60,000 people on the Mississippi River. The meat packing company was huge –with 3,000 employees. The family took me in very well. Mrs. Wahlert was a very nice woman and she treated me like another of her children. Bob, the eldest son, was studying at the University of Iowa. Dave, the second son, was studying in town and he liked basketball so we played together. In August 1960 the Olympic Games were being held in Rome. We were all following the event on TV.

Change of Plans

In mid-September 1960, Alberto Muller called me to tell me that Cuban college students in Miami had created the Student Revolutionary Directorate (Directorio Revolucionario Estudiantil, DRE) with the stated goal of uniting all students in the fight against Fidel Castro's dictatorship as part of the Democratic Revolutionary Front (Frente Revolucionario Democrático, FDR). We agreed to meet in New York on September 27th. From Dubuque I returned to Chicago staying once again at the Palmer Hotel. One afternoon, while strolling near the, I passed the nearby Hilton Hotel. Soon the typical sirens of police patrol cars were heard. Some were shouting: "It's the presidential candidate! Aboard one of the patrol cars was John F. Kennedy and he stopped right in front of me on his way to the Hilton while shaking hands with the crowd. A very tall policeman approached me and asked who I was and what was I doing there. That evening, I watched on T.V. the famous debate between Kennedy and Nixon. Kennedy outdid his adversary according to what I read in the newspapers the following day. It is obvious that at that time I knew almost nothing about U.S. politics.

On September 27th I went to New York to attend the meeting we agreed. Alberto Muller came with Miguelón García Armengol and Juan Manuel Salvat. This meeting was crucial for me: it changed my plans and my life. Up to then I had decided to finish my studies, since as a professional I would be able to be of greater use to a Cuba free of Castro. A priest in Dubuque had impressed on me that my country needed honest and capable professionals.

Alberto, on the other hand, brought me terrible news to New York. My good friend from childhood in the neighborhood and later at ACU, Carlos Rodríguez Santana, had fallen off from the top of a mountain in Guatemala and died while training in the camps to invade Cuba. His badge number was 2506, later this number would become famous.

Julián had been murdered and Carlos had died, how could I continue my studies as if nothing had happened? Really, I didn't feel in peace with my own conscience. Alberto asked me to return to Cuba to organize the Student Directorate there, together with the friends who had participated in the event at Havana's Central Park. I accepted.

Having made my decision, I had to go back to the University of Chicago to cancel the first quarter toward the Master's Degree –since my father had already paid for it– and to pick up my Economics books to send them to Miami. When I commented my decision to a staff worker, and explained my reasons, his reaction was to tell me: "You are crazy."

Finally I got to Miami. I was met by Juan Manuel Salvat and Ernesto Fernández Travieso. In Miami I visited my aunt Kika and her husband. I also visited an old friend, Rafael Rivas Vázquez. He was in charge of recruiting volunteers for the training camps in Guatemala. Rafael told me that so far there were 187 men and invited me to join them in Guatemala while explaining that the plan called for a group of experts to infiltrate Cuba and establish guerilla action hubs. At that time the idea was not to invade the island. I declined the invitation because I had already given my word to the Student Directorate. Alberto was away on a trip and as soon as he got back we agreed upon the work I had to undertake in Cuba.

$$= \circ = \circ = \circ =$$

The Underground

I arrived in Havana on October 7, 1960 and entered normally through the airport. Alberto, Miguelón, Salvat and Ernesto were to arrive later. Ernesto had recommended that I talk to his brother Tomás to drive me around in his car to run the errands assigned to me. First of all, I headed to see my cousin Eddy Crews who had come with me to the *Sierra* as part of the Literacy Corps in 1959. Eddy had married and was expecting his first child with his wife Gemma. I began to make my contacts. I also spoke with Father Llorente. Many of the friends I talked to thought that there would be an invasion from abroad at any moment. I explained to them that that was not the current plan, that in Guatemala there were less than 200 men.

I tried to make contact with all the student organizations of the Democratic Revolutionary Front, the MRR (Movimiento de Recuperación Revolucionaria), the Christian Democrats and the Auténticos. There was a great deal of excitement among the students against the dictatorship that was beginning to take hold with abso-

47

lute control. One of them was Luis Fernández Rocha, leader of the student section of the MRR. I was able to speak directly with Rogelio González Corso (pseudonym: Francisco). He was the person in charge of the Democratic Revolutionary Front in Cuba and he suggested that I travel outside the island capital to incorporate students from the provinces. In that mission I was accompanied by another fellow from the Literacy Corps: Jorge "El Pico" Marbán. We travelled to Oriente by car and there I established contact with Father Méndez, a Jesuit from the *Dolores* School. I stopped by Holguín to visit Father Jorge Bez Chabebe who had fought in the *Sierra Maestra* with Fidel Castro. The priest took me to the parish bell tower to ensure privacy; then he confessed that he was against the process undertaken by Fidel Castro but that he disagreed with how the resistance was being organized.

In Camagüey I was met by two student leaders of the city high school: Gustavo Caballero and José Bernando "Chicho" González, both very interested in organizing the high school students. In Sagua la Grande, I contacted Rafael Marqués (affectionately known as Marquesito), and José "Puchi" González, very well-known at Santa Clara High School. In Matanzas my efforts did not yield any results, so I finally returned to Havana.

I didn't want to let my parents know about my return to Cuba. However, at this time I asked a good friend of the family to bring over my mother so I could see her, perhaps for the last time. He brought her my cousin Eddy's home for the meeting. My mother's surprise was unimaginable. She started crying while telling me that I was going to get killed. We talked for a while about her own plans. My father was counting on her to leave Cuba first to prepare the way and buy a house. He intended to follow suit later, on December 15, 1960, to settle permanently in Miami.

My mother's visit devastated me. Seeking spiritual help I headed to Pius XII, a house of spiritual exercises in La Coronela area, on the outskirts of Havana. I went on retreat from November 16th to the 20th. I still recall clearly what was for me a culminating reflection: Jesus is at the Mount of Olives praying to his father: "He went a little farther, and fell on his knees, and prayed, O my Father, if possible, let this cup pass away from me: nevertheless let it be done according to Thy will" (Matthew 26:39). This is how I felt. I could not see the end of the struggle against Fidel Castro since he still enjoyed great backing from the general population, as I was able to ascertain from my trip through the country. On Sunday the 20th the retreat ended. Among the participants was Modesto Alonso, and old schoolmate from Belén.

On Sunday, at the end of the retreat, Father Llorente told me that Alberto Muller had arrived in Cuba and that Rogelio González Corzo (Francisco) needed help on a mission. I was excited about this. That evening my old friend Hugo Díaz brought me to his house to color my hair black since the bright blond I wore attracted attention.

The following day he took me to Luis Fernández Rocha's house where I was introduced to José Octavio "El Chino" Guzmán Peña. He was in charge of taking me to the Escambray Mountains in the Province of Las Villas. *El Chino* had been born and raised in the Escambray and had been part of Che Guevara's guerillas there, as well as a member of the Catholic Labor Youth (Juventud Obrera Católica, JOC). He impressed me as very capable and trustworthy so I accepted to go with him. He told me that a few days before he had returned from the Escambray –where the guerillas were operating– and that he had prepared a map of the place where an airplane could drop weapons from Guatemala. The date selected was November 30, 1960. They would be caught by guerillas loyal to *El Chino* and members of the MRR organization in the city of Cienfuegos. Said map was sent to Guatemala through the U.S. Embassy in Cuba.

I wanted to meet with Alberto Muller who was already in town. So I was taken to a house in the Miramar district of Havana. Luis Fernández Rocha was also there. Everything was ready for the founding of the Student Revolutionary Directorate

(Directorio Revolucionario Estudiantil, DRE) on Cuban soil. I was excited, especially because I had been promised a radio transmitter to take to the Escambray. I was thinking of installing a radio station in the mountains which was very needed –just like Fidel Castro had done with his Rebel Radio at the Sierra Maestra. Also, the news broadcasted from Miami by Radio Swan were not trustworthy. Alberto was not in agreement but Luis was. We were talking about the possibility of opening a DRE front against Castro from the Escambray. Later on other members would follow. I handed to Alberto a list of contacts that I had established during my tour of the provinces. He had plans to keep in touch with them.

Off to the Escambray

On Monday, November 21, 1960, El Chino Guzmán and I left for Cienfuegos. Once there, we stayed at different locations. We got info that State Security was very active in the area as many of the members that were planning to join the insurrection in the Escambray had been arrested. On the 24th I was moved to another house where I joined with El Chino. He told me that apparently we had been betrayed by an informant and that we had to flee town. They loaned us a car and we left by way of the Southern Circuit road towards Colón, in Matanzas, to merge with the Central Highway. But soon, before getting to Colón we saw at a distance a car full of government soldiers in hot pursuit. The car pulled ahead of us blocking us off. Three soldiers emerged with machine guns demanding we come out from the car. They spoke to my companion: "we finally grabbed you Chino, you are under arrest." I thought they did not know about me, Besides, I was carrying on me a signed document (supposedly from my father's company) that identified me as a merchandise salesman. Of course, none of us could imagine that the government informant who had infiltrated the ranks of the MRR in Cienfuegos was Benigno Balsa Batista, who knew us perfectly well.

The soldiers took us to the headquarters of the State Security in Las Villas, on the outskirts of the capital city of Santa Clara. They placed us in separate cells. The following day, November 25th, they took me out of my cell for interrogation. The welcoming was: "You know we are going to execute you. You are the delegate of the Frente Revolucionario Democrático." I did not reply at all and they took me back to my cell, one of six that had recently been built in back of an old house on a secondary road near the center of town. There was only one bathroom in the hallway. Long days began for me in prayer inside the cell, in preparation to face a firing squad. I was interrogated every day. On the third day Benigno Balsa Batista, the infiltrated informant, was waiting for me, dressed in the uniform of the regime's militiamen. He sat in front of me with a machine gun in his lap. He starting by telling me why his betrayal had saved my because if I had reached the mountains the militia would have killed us as they had done with the rest. Of course I did not believe a word he was saying. The interrogation stopped when I confessed that I was in Cienfuegos to join the guerilla in the Escambray. They made me put everything in writing. Part of it was: "My conscience is at rest with God and with the Fatherland."

On the sixth day of confinement they authorized me to call my family to tell them where I was being held prisoner. Despite the distance from Havana, the following day, my beloved nanny from childhood Chacha came to see me. She was still employed with the family and was living in my parents' house. My father came later. He seemed weak, even sick. My mom was in the U.S. as they had planned before all this happened.

Raúl Álvarez Cabarga, a member of the ACU I had previously met, had been arrested and brought into my cell. It was a relief to be able to pray the rosary together.

Early in December the guards brought to our cell two other young prisoners. They told us they attacked a military garrison in Trinidad and had been arrested while trying to join the guerillas in the Escambray Mountains. While already under the custody of

Castro soldiers, a gun battle had nsued between the soldiers and other guerillas. When the battle ended, the soldiers realized that the Commander-in-Chief of Castro's troups in the Escambray –and former member of Castro's troups in the Sierra Maestra– Dr. Piti Fajardo, was dead, a victim of friendly fire from his own troops which had been able to circle around the whole area. Of course, the circumstances surrounding his death were never revealed by the Castro regime, and scapegoats were useful.

Other prisoners were brought to the cells. These had been captured while trying to highjack a commercial airplane in flight, and take it to Miami. There had been a shoot-out, but the pilot was able to land on Cuban soil before dying.

A few days later my mother was back from the U.S. and, together with my father came to visit me. My mom brought me the Eucharist hidden in her bosom. That night Cabarga and I shared the host and both us prayed the rosary to our Mother Mary, the Immaculate Conception. We offered up our lives to Christ because we thought we would be executed.

The night of December 7, 1960 I was taken to another cell. This one I shared with Eloy Moreno –one of the airplane assailants– and with one of the men who had participated in the events in Trinidad and the Escambray. Both had already gone through a trial and condemned to death. I had not. That night two soldiers told them that their appeals had been refused and that they would be executed the following day: December 8th, on the festivity of the Immaculate Conception. This place had become a death row. We spent most of the night praying the rosary.

The guards allowed a Protestant Pastor to spiritually prepare those to be executed. With my pre-Vatican II Council's mentality I protested that he was not a Catholic priest. Eloy Moreno agreed to talk to the Pastor. They were only able to talk for a few minutes through the cell bars. The next morning eight men were taken out their cells and taken to *La Campana*, a place selected for the firing squad executions at that time.

It is important to mention that the Government conducted "trials" and executions as means of threat and retribution, not following a legal procedure in Court. There were disproportionate sentences handed out without evidence, and therefore, unfair.

The Trial

A week after these unforgettable events happened, all the members of my case were moved to a prison in the province capital, Santa Clara. We were at ease thinking that we were out of danger of been executed under these horrible circumstances. There, we found thirty persons, all captured by agent Benigno Balsa Batista. My parents allowed to visit me again. In early February 1961 we got a big surprise: we were going to trial.

The "trial" was open to the public at the Provincial Courtroom. Our family members were present. The government brought out an exhibit of a Nazi flag and weapons supposedly captured by their soldiers and militia dropped by airplane in a failed attempt to supply anti-government guerillas.

The Prosecutor was asking a 30-year sentence for the leader and 20 and 15 for the rest. They didn't ask for the death penalties. The Chief of the State Security accused those he thought had undertaken the most serious activities against the Revolution. We were thinking the Prosecutor would reconsider and ask for a harsher penalty, but that was not the case. On February 3, 1961 I was sentenced to 30 years in prison under Case #51/61. Mother Mary had protected me during the whole ordeal.

On February 5th, exactly one year to the day after the demonstrations in Havana's Central Park, we were transferred by the Cuban Air Force to the Isle of Pines, south of the Province of Havana.

Thus, my First World came to an end.

Personal photos

**MY GRANDFATHER – THOMAS D. CREWS
MY GRANDMOTHER – SOFIA CARRERA
MY MOTHER –CARMEN CREWS
MY AUNT – MERCEDES CREWS
MY UNCLE – JOE CREWS**

MY PARENTS – ANTONIO GARCIA CERVANTES / CARMEN CREWS
MY GODFATHER – EMILIO CERVANTES
MY AUNT – CARMEN CERVANTES

MY PARENTS
ANTONIO GARCIA CERVANTES
CARMEN CREWS

**COLEGIO DE BELÉN
WHERE I GRADUATED FROM HIGH SCHOOL**

**TRACK TEAM – CHAMPIONS 1956
COLEGIO BELÉN, HABANA, CUBA**

COLEGIO DE BELÉN
UNDER 15
CHAMPIONS IN THE INTER SCHOOL LEAGUE

**FRESHMEN ROWING TEAM AT THE HABANA YACHT CLUB
1956**

**FOUR GREAT FRIENDS COURSE OF 1957. COLEGIO BELÉN, HABANA, CUBA
(from left to right)
José Ramy-Alvarez
Antonio García-Crews
Joaquín Pérez: President "Instituto Pedro Arrupe"
Julián Martínez-Inclán: Martyr December 28, 1958**

Antonio García, desarrolló el tema: "La Moral y la Educación".

ANTONIO GARCIA
DEVELOPED THE THESIS: MORAL AND EDUCATION

THE BELEN GRADUATES AHEAD OF THE FUTURE OF CUBA

GRADUATION IN COLEGIO BELEN
JUNE 14, 1957

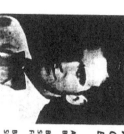

CLASS OF 2016

Antonio García-Crews
Class of 1957
Basketball, Baseball, and Track & Field

Athletic:
Belen Athlete of the Year (1957)

Basketball
Starter 1956 & 1957 Under 18 Team - Center and Forward; Starter 1954 & 1955 Under 15 Team - 2 Undefeated Seasons - Ce
Forward

Baseball
Starter 1956 & 1957 Under 18 Team - First Baseman; Starter 1954 & 1955 Under 15 Team - First Baseman

Track and Field
Javelin (1954-1957) Set School Record in 1954 at the age of 15; Member of the 4x50 Champion Relay Team (1954-1955)

Professional and Personal:
Member of the Florida Bar since 1992; Member of the American Immigration Lawyers Assoc.; Since 1992, has defended more than 500 political asylum seeke
before the US courts; Approximately 300 cases taken on a pro-bono basis to represent needy clients.
Political Prisoner for 16 years in Cuba (1960-1976)

Lives in Altamonte Springs, FL with his wife, Maria Elena García.

Advice to young athletes:
Select a sport you really like and persevere in the hard work toward success.

How do you feel being part of the Belen Sports Hall of Fame Class of 2016?
I feel very honored and grateful for this recognition which I want to share with my class of 1957, my family and friends that made this possible.

RECOGNITION IN COLEGIO BELEN BEST ATHLETE OF THE COURSE 1957

MIAMI, FLORIDA

**WITH THE RURAL COMMANDOS OF THE MINISTRY OF AGRICULTURE
IN "LA SIERRA MAESTRA"
ORIENTE, CUBA 1959**

IN JAIL AFTER THE DEMOSTRATION
AGAINST ANASTAS MIKOYAN
FEBRUARY 5, 1960

**FAREWELL LETTER TO MY PARENTS INFORMING THEM
THAT I WAS NOT GOING TO CONTINUE MY STUDIES
AT THE UNIVERSITY OF CHICAGO
SEPTEMBER 27, 1960**

LETTER TO MY PARENTS

Chicago, September 27, 1960

Dear parents,

I have tried for several days to write this letter, but I have not found the moment or the means to do it. All I am saying here I should have said it in Havana some time ago, but my will power is weak and the love I have for you was stronger than Christ's call to fulfill my duty.

Mom, you will understand all this better, you know the struggle between opposite feelings inside my soul for some time. Do you remember the day I took you to my Spiritual Director to talk to him?

Now, I can unequivocally say that Christ has won over my soul, the same way he did when he took me to the "Congregación", where I said "no" to the terrible life I had led up to that moment; like that time after my initiation when He asked me to go fight in La Sierra Maestra Mountains which did not happen because of the fall of Batista's dictatorship. Then later on when we volunteered to work with the peasants, and afterwards at Havana University, etc. – besides every other time you know about since you lived through it. Even when some times you actively opposed it, Christ's will always triumphed.

Today, I can't fail to remember the Bible story about the child lost and found in the temple: Jesus was lost, his parents did not know where he was. He was making them suffer horribly – the Son of God disobeyed his parents! When he was finally found, he was told: "Son, why did you not tell us, your disobedience has made us suffer". He responded: "Because I was taking care of business for my Father in heaven".

I visited the University of Chicago –which I liked a lot, by the way- and cancelled my admission and boarding for another time. They understood and told me I would be admitted to any other semester I may ask for. You were in my mind more than ever and I only answered: "because I have to take care of my father's business who is in heaven and his will is that us Catholics have to be witnesses that He exists and is justice "the way, the truth, e the life". This, taken to its ultimate consequences.

In these circumstances, I remember my father, whom I love more than ever, and pray to God for him so he understands that Tony is no longer his child, he is now a man with responsibilities he can't refuse – that would be treason to God himself whose early appearances in life's grave problems I was never worried about – the meetings held in Belen with Father Camacho when I returned home stating: "our children's fatherland either we build it or nobody will". You laughed when I talked about social reforms and justice for the oppressed long before the powerful Fidel Castro did. Dad, you used to say that all that was impossible. Less than one year after, others did try to make those ideals a reality but without our principles.

I did not wish to talk to you about this to save you from worrying – not until I could reach the irrevocable decision of not attending the university. Bob Whalert was of great help because he assumed a father's duty during the most difficult times in my life.

I was in New York last Friday & Saturday and could meet Ernesto and others. That was all I needed to make a decision. The Congregation Hymn goes like this:

"Christ suffered a redemptive cross, Cuba has the light of a star.
Let's raise the star toward heaven, and plant the Cross in our land".

Julian Martinez learned to plant very well.

Mom, I suffered a lot when you told me about Dad's intention to leave home if he failed to convince me I had to return to the United States. I never thought my father respected my freedom so little. The same freedom God respects, even when we greatly offend Him. Of course, I understood your point, Dad, because pressures were too great and you have always wished and given the best in the world to me.

I won't quit my studies and promise to return to them as soon as possible. For me, not studying at a prestigious university is the greatest sacrifice of my life. But, to save us, Christ was willing to die on a cross for our sins..... what would I not accomplish for Him, the most generous Son that ever existed !

You may wish to follow me or something like that, but I beg you not to try it for the safety of all. I am going to see Mercy today. She will know what to tell you when you each time you call.

My spiritual director will give you some information, I guess, regarding my ideals. He does not yet know about the university, but he could guess it would happen.

Let's now forget Christ in the Olive Garden on the vigil of his Passion. His words, "Father, if possible, let this cup pass away from me, but may Your will be done, not Mine". However, when all seemed lost for his disciples and with no chance of salvation, in the darkest moment, the Son of Man resurrected. That is our guarantee of triumph, no matter how big and strong our enemy is.

You can be sure that the only thing that moves me to make this decision is the assurance that I am fulfilling the Will of God. He will give me enough grace to follow Him. I wish to have you by my side in this moment of triumph, but we will soon be together. The Blessed Mother, our Virgin, wishes this,too.

I ask you once again to keep secret all about the university. Only tell my spiritual father and Eddy – nobody else. As you may understand, my son's heart would like to tell you much more.

Long live Christ the King,
I love you more every day,

Tony

P.D. Big hugs to Chacha, aunt Carmen, Chelo and the Silvarios –always happy.

"Look at me, Mother, and don't cry out of love for me. If my youth and my doctrines your martyr heart have crowned with thorns; just think that that flowers grow among thorns".   José Martí

En reunión celebrada el día 5 de octubre de 1960 en la ciudad de Miami, el Ejecutivo del DIRECTORIO REVOLUCIONARIO ESTUDIANTIL, acuerda:

Nombrar coordinador del Directorio en el Clandestinaje al compañero Alejandro (nombre de guerra). Este se pondrá en contacto con los compañeros que en este momento luchan para derrocar la dictadura comunista instaurada en nuestra Patria y desarrollará perfectamente la organización final del Directorio en el clandestinaje. Se encargará además de desarrollar las otras labores que le asignen el ejecutivo en el exilio.

Por el Ejecutivo del DIRECTORIO REVOLUCIONARIO ESTUDIANTIL del F. R. D.

Secretario General
Alberto Müller

Secretario de Relaciones Publicas
Abel de Varona

Secretario de Propaganda

Secretario de Inteligencia y Comunicaciones
Oscar Orallo

Secretario de Actas y Correspondencia
Alejandro Portes

Secretario de Asuntos Militares
Ernesto Fernández-Travieso

Secretario de Organización
Jorge Mas Canosa

Secretario de Finanzas
Tulio Díaz

Secretaria de Asuntos Femeninos
Teresita Valdes-Hurtado

Secretario de Asuntos Pre-Universitarios

**ALEJANDRO WAS ASSIGNED "CHOSEN PSEUDONYM"
TO COORDINATE THE CREATION OF THE
REVOLUCIONARY STUDENT DIRECTORY IN CUBA
OCTOBER 5, 1960**

STUDENTS REVOLUTIONARY DIRECTORY

During a meeting held on the 5th day of October, 1960, in the city of Miami, the Board of the STUDENTS REVOLUTIONARY DIRECTORY decided to name our partner Alejandro (chosen pseudonym) as the Underground Coordinator of this Directory.

He is assigned to contact other members who are already fighting to overthrow the communist dictatorship established in our fatherland; and to develop this section in the underground to its final shape. He will also perform other responsibilities assigned to him by the Executive in exile.

Signed by Executive members of the D.R.E.

General Secretary	Alberto Muller
Public Relations Secretary	Abel de Varona
Propaganda Secretary	Juan Manuel Salvat
Intelligence & Communications	Oscar Cerallo
Official Documents & Correspondence	Alejandro Portes
Military Affairs Secretary	Ernesto Fernandez Travieso
Organizational Secretary	Jorge Más Canosa
Finance Secretary	Tulio Diaz
Women's Affairs Secretary	Teresita Valdes Hurtado
College preps' Secretary	Carlos de Varona

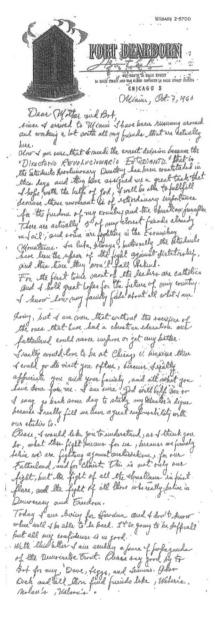

**FAREWELL LETTER TO THE WAHLERT FAMILY,
DAY OF MY RETURN TO CUBA TO ORGANIZE
THE REVOLUTIONARY STUDENT DIRECTORY
OCTOBER 7, 1960**

LETTER TO THE WAHLERTS

Miami, October 7, 1960

Dear Mother and Bob,

Since I arrived to Miami, I have been running around and working a lot with all my friends that are actually here. Now, I am sure that I made the correct decision because the "DIRECTORIO REVOLUCIONARIO ES-TUDIANTIL" –that is, the "Students Revolutionary Directory"– has been constituted in these days and they have assigned me a great task that I hope, with the help of God, I will be able to fulfill because this movement is of extraordinary importance for the freedom of my country and the Christian principles. There are actually 5 of my closest friends already in jail, and some are fighting in the *Escambray* mountains.

In Cuba always, historically, the students have been the spear of the fight against dictatorship and this time they won't fall behind. For the first time most of the leaders are Catholics and I hold great hopes for the future of my country.

I know how my family feels about all I am doing, but I am sure that without the sacrifice of the ones that have had a Christian education, our fatherland could never improve or get any better.

I really would love to be at Chicago University because then I could go to visit you often because I really appreciate you and your family and all that you have done for me. I am sure God will help me so I may go back some day to study for my Master's degree. I really feel we have a great re-sponsibility with our studies too.

Please, I would like you to understand –as I think you do– what this fight means for us because we firmly believe we are fighting against mate-rialism, for our fatherland, and for Christ. This is not only our fight, but the fight of all the Christians in first place, and the fight of all those who really believe in democracy and freedom.

Today, I am leaving for Havana and I don't know when will I be able to be back. It is going to be difficult but all my confidence is in God.

With this letter, I am sending a pair of propaganda of the Democratic Front.

Please, say good-by to Bob for me, Dave, Tiggs and Jeannie. Also Dick and all those fine friends like Weheris, Nolan, Nelson.

Tony

SECOND
WORLD

*"I remembered Merton's line about the monastery
being the four walls to my freedom"*
James Martin S.J. (America Magazine June 2021)

SECOND WORLD

My arrival at the Isle of Pines was catastrophic. It was very cold. The prison guards had taken the 30 members of Cause #51 of 1961 who had come with me to the 6th floor of Circular Building 4. In the middle of the building there was a watchtower from which the guards were able to keep an eye on anything that moved. The first five floors consisted of cells numbered 1 to 90, but the 6th floor was not divided by walls. The ground floor was a concrete flat area with cold water showers protruding from the walls: all in all we were 1,000 prisoners.

We were welcomed by companions and friends who had been sent there previously. They had with them some blankets and covers used in sleeping on the floor, as the building was filled beyond capacity. Somebody lent me a blanket and I wrapped myself with it, got down to the concrete floor and fell asleep. I slept for a long time and when I woke up it still felt impossible to be experiencing what I was living. So many events had taken place so quickly: the last days of the Batista regime, the assassination of my friend Julián, Castro's entrance in Havana, his promise of holding elections in 90 days, the change in direction that events had taken; my early enthusiasm, my stay at the Sierra Maestra teaching peasants, the reopening of universities, the protests at the Central Park in Havana; Chicago, Dubuque, New York, Miami, and my return to Havana; the underground conspiracy, my arrest, the State Security in Las Villas, the death in Guatemala of Carlos Rodriguez Santana (#2506), executions by firing squad, the prefabricated trials of all the members of my case – something I would have never been able to imagine – and now here I was sleeping on a cement floor on a cold night in the p

rison of the Isle of Pines, to the south of the Province of Havana.

Another fellow inmate gave me a small round aluminum dish where to put the food that they were distributing in the ground floor. Everything was a mystery to be discovered. They gave us a yellowish uniform similar to the one Batista soldiers wore. Little by little I began to discover how things worked in that place, and who would be the players. Every day we would get packages of food and clothing sent by our families. The canteen food was prepared by family members of the inmates who lived in the Isle of Pines. My parents pulled off getting me a food ration on my second day.

Little by little the inmates from the first to the fifth floor provided us with accommodations inside their cells. Five days later a friend from the days of the underground, Manolo Villanueva, invited me to stay at his cell with another prisoner –I would be the third. I would no longer have to sleep on the barren floor; my parents had sent me a sort of canvass cot that folded in half.

I began to realize that more than half of the prison population had been connected one way or another with Batista's army (soldiers and officers). There were also guerillas captured at the Escambray Mountains who had fought against Castro. At that point in time I thought that the resistance to Castro in Cuba (especially in the Escambray, Pinar del Río and the Sierra Maestra in Oriente) would continue to grow and strengthen, and that in the end Castro would be defeated. Talking to my friends I found out that the Student Directorate was gaining supporters and that they had called for a student strike at the national level.

Castro had still not declared himself a Communist, but his actions spoke for themselves: the confiscation of the sugar mills and of most private businesses –for example, my father's. The first few months of 1961 (January to April) went by. The inmates had a crystal radio receiver hidden from the guards by means of which we would find out about the most important news broadcast by the Voice of America. On April 15th a bombardment of the Columbia Military Base took place; and on the 17th, early in the morning, we were awakened by machinegun bursts from placements on hilltops near the prison because an invading airplane was coming through the area. Some of Batista's soldiers began to cry out "Viva Batista" while the guards began to fire against them from the outside. Our group of prisoners didn't know anything about what was going on, only rumors of a landing in Cuba. Days later we found out that there had been a small invasion that had failed and that most of the attackers were dead or in prison. Visits by our family members to the penitentiary were suspended (until June) and we had no way to communicate with them.

Gradually we began to get more news about the disaster. The government had jailed many citizens (maybe thousands) in stadiums and in prisons, afraid that an internal resistance movement might take hold. Rogelio González Corso had been captured and shot by firing squad. Tommy Fernández Travieso was in jail and Alberto Muller had been captured in the Province of Oriente leading an insurgency. The Isle of Pines was for us a desert, devoid of any hope for a quick return to freedom. The prison guards had dynamited during the days of the invasion the building where we were held so that if there were to be a rescue attempted they would blow up the place.

$$= \circ = \circ = \circ =$$

After the failure of Girón (Bay of Pigs) it was time for the formation of men looking ahead to a future Cuba, which we thought would come sooner or later. I joined up with Octavio Guzmán, my buddy when we had tried to join the rebels at the Escambray, who had been held in prison since then. Octavio was a member of the Juventud Obrera Católica (JOC, Catholic Workers Youth) who wanted to train young prisoners regarding principles and ideals. We began small meetings on the sixth floor of Building 4, the only open space in the building where we were. The small group began to grow and Guzmán invited me to teach classes on the Social Doctrine of the Church, something I had studied extensively.

I began the classes with the basic principles: the dignity of the human person, the common good, social justice and private property in its social aspect. It is interesting how, among all these concepts, the one that garnered the most interest was social justice. Perhaps it was due to the fact that at that time Cuba was in a revolution that had described itself as a democracy, but which had deviated its course toward totalitarianism.

But the concepts of Christian Social Doctrine were our principles and we continued to believe that it was necessary to recuperate the revolution from the hands of Communists to put social justice in practice. We did not accept being called counter-revolutionaries because we believed that a democratic revolution, respectful of social justice, was feasible.

Evidently, to pose these topics in the midst of a majority of prisoners who had been part of the Batista military was dangerous. The sad part was that other prisoners, not related to the Batista regime, began to accuse us, JOC young guys, of teaching Communist doctrine. When I found out about the accusation I felt deeply offended. Many of the ones spreading these lies were planning to take up important positions in a new government once Castro had been defeated, and so they thought it necessary to suppress us.

We kept on going with our training sessions for the guys, ignoring their attacks. The JOC group kept on growing. As time went by other prisoners began to arrive from other groups allied to the Student Directorate, such as the MRR, MRP and the Christian Democrats, all were organizations belonging to the Democratic Revolutionary Front and the Revolutionary Council headed by

Miró Cardona, who Fidel Castro had named as Prime Minister at the start of his revolution.

The failure of the Bay of Pigs invasion and the capture of hundreds of participants who were fighting for political democracy, as well as the multiple executions by firing squad inside prison created great confusion and disappointment. I was convinced and held on to the hope that the work we were doing with the JOC in training Christian men would be important for the future of Cuba.

During 1961, my first year in prison, I was held still at Building 4. Serious arguments with former Batista military were to continue (their favorite phrase was: "you put them there, you bring them down.") At the end of the year the worst possible thing took place. A Batista-era prisoner who had acted as Major was taken down and another inmate from our group was elected Major. This was the prisoner in charge of communications with the prison staff in order to give out their orders and to let the staff know about any petitions from the prisoners. The government was following the policy of keeping the Batista military together with the other prisoners like me who had fought on the side of the revolution. Its purpose was to provoke conflicts and incidents to then intervene and punish us with much-feared inspections: whereby all prisoners were forced into the ground floor of the prison (in their underwear) to stand up while the guards would throw away all of their belongings.

We had the first visit with our families in June of the year. It was Christmastime but they did not allow them to send us any food – only those packages of food they authorized.

In 1962 a large number of transfers among buildings took place. I was sent from Building 4 to 1. Of course, transferring with our scant belongings and not knowing where we were headed was extremely hard on us causing great consternation. I was lucky to meet up with a great friend from college, Ricardo Sarabasa, who was jailed during the invasion. We had studied Economics together at the University of Villanueva and we continued our studies in the cell with books that our families would send us and which the guards had allowed us to receive.

In building 1, I found many old acquaintances from the struggle and the underground, to the point that the Batista military became a minority. My group and I would meet with other study groups covering other subjects. Miguelón García Armengol, Mundito Torres and I decided to study French. At the same time, I pledged to teach English and catechism. The news from the outside world that we would get via our hidden radio was disappointing: resistance to the revolution inside Cuba was extinguishing.

Up to that time we had two priests imprisoned in our building with us. When Alberto Muller got there with a group of more men, two other priests came in. Masses were being held in secret on the sixth floor behind blankets that we would put up –supposedly to dry out– so the guards would not detect us.

Once family visits had resumed packages of dry milk and other types of food were received to supplement jail rations that were getting worse and worse. Towards the end of the summer the situation was becoming unbearable. On September 8, 1962, the feast of Our Lady of Charity, we declared a hunger strike with the support of all four buildings of the Isle of Pines Model Penitentiary. We rejected all food rations, drinking only water. Later, approximately ten days later, we woke up surrounded by at least 500 Rebel Army soldiers armed with bazookas and including tanks. The garrison commander informed the Major that they were there to conduct a "peaceful inspection" (hence known for history as "La Pacífica"). We were all made to walk down to the ground floor in our underwear only, under threat of bombarding the building, beginning with the sixth floor to ensure that nobody would escape compliance with the order. Once everyone had come down the soldiers entered our cells throwing out everything they found from the highest floor down. They only left behind the canvas cots. All the little we had by way of possessions that allowed us to survive: food, clothing, mattresses, books, ended up in the middle of the ground floor. We lost everything. After this monstrosity we had no choice but to start eating again, all the while fearing that they would end up killing us all.

For some time now, we had been hearing sounds from the basement which had us intrigued and disconcerted. Now we could identify them as jack hammers opening holes in the tunnels under the building where we were being held. When they had finished opening the holes they filled them with plastic TNT. That way they dynamited all the buildings. The unthinkable was taking place.

A few days later we found out through the Voice of America that Russian nuclear weapons had been detected in Cuba and evidence of it was presented before the United Nations Assembly. Also, that President Kennedy had ordered a naval blockade around the Island. That was the reason for the dynamite under us. They would have blasted us if an invasion or another action against the government had been launched.

On Saturday, October 27, 1962, during the vigil of Christ the King, Father Rojo celebrated Mass on the sixth floor. We thought it would be the last one of our lives. But, to our surprise, and that of the whole world, the following morning the Prime Minister of the Soviet Union sent a letter to the President of the United States informing him that he would remove his nuclear missiles from Cuba (while the U.S. would remove its missile sites in Turkey was later known). That is how the worst crisis in the history of humanity would end.

Apparently we all learned a lesson: playing war games is not to be done on planet Earth. We are all vulnerable. Towards the end of December 1962, after a long drawn out negotiation that included food donations to Cuba, the prisoners jailed since the Bay of Pigs invasion in April 1961 were sent back to the United States.

= o = o = o =

The year 1963 brought me some important and hopeful news. James Donovan, a New York lawyer whose good offices had brought about the positive result of setting free the Bay of Pigs prisoners was engaged this time in trying to liberate the prisoners among us who were U.S. citizens. From the U.S., my family was able to get me included in this group based on the fact that my grandfather, Thomas Crews, born in Georgia, had registered all his grandchildren as American citizens at the U.S. Embassy since birth. I was happy at the news but also sad as I would be the only one among my friends to enjoy this privilege. During the month of April the release and transfer of more than 20 American prisoners was undertaken by the Cuban government. However, I was not allowed to leave. Why? Attorney Donovan explained to my family in the United States that the Cuban government did not consent to consider me to be an American citizen, and that therefore, I had been taken off the list. Donovan promised to continue his efforts to get the job done. This never came to pass.

On November 22, 1963, in the afternoon, while I was walking around the second floor of building 1 at the penitentiary, a friend of mine came out of his cell, where we hid the crystal radio receiver that kept us informed, to tell me that President Kennedy had been assassinated. Obviously, these news were a hard blow for all of us. At that time I had been thinking that once the Bay of Pigs and American prisoners had been negotiated, it was possible for the rest of the prisoners to be freed as well someday. This hope was not totally baseless: years later we found out that an emissary of Kennedy, Jean Danielou had been exploring a possible reestablishment of diplomatic relations between the two countries.

$$= \circ = \circ = \circ =$$

In 1964 several events took place that affected our situation. The jail authorities decided to build a sort of huge mesh cage, such that from there on family visits would take place from either side of the fencing. The spontaneous and unanimous reaction of the prisoners was totally against accepting visits under these conditions. So we ended up with no visits. On the other hand, we knew that resistance to the regime had dissipated due to the brutal repression, although really we were getting very little news about any type of resistance.

We continued to train men of conscience coming from groups of inmates members of various anti-Castro movements. My knowledge of the French language was now enough to allow me to read books in that language, and a better chance to avoid censorship.

We were studying History, Economics and the Social Doctrine of the Church. Our families sent us two Encyclicals by Pope John XXIII: Mater et Magistra (Mother and Teacher) and Pacem in Terris (Peace on Earth). We would get together to read and discuss them. It was a sort of university behind bars. This created an additional separation inside the prison population: those of us that took time to study to train with a view of the future and those who took to playing cards or dominoes to pass the time. A friend and fellow inmate conducted an important analysis which he called "The New Reality." It was a conscience raising exercise about the deep changes established by the Cuban government in order to adopt its totalitarian system –an awakening to the reality that the future loomed different from how the past had been. This contributed to new prisoners joining the group with various perspectives and fresh views of what was in fact taking place.

Towards the end of 1964 we found out that the government had planned to set up forced labor in the penitentiary. It was to be called "Camilo Cienfuegos Work Plan." It consisted in setting up work details teams of 20-30 inmates surrounded by soldiers and controlled by an armed guard. The prisoners opposed the plan because its purpose was to destroy the morale and ideals of the men, forcing them to accept Marxist-Leninist ideology implemented by the government throughout Cuba. A long tradition against this plan was already in existence since the failure of the Bay of Pigs.

Before forced labor was to start our Bloc of Revolutionary Organizations (grouping together prisoners coming from the Directorate, the MRR, the MRP, the Christian Democrats and the Auténticos) had prepared a long document, signed by everyone, in which we stated that to volunteer to do hard labor was Treason for us.

In September the plan began with building 1. I was assigned to block 19, which grouped students. The first day of work we were taken to a quarry. The guard in charge of my work gang took me out of the group, conducted me to a hole and began to beat me his machete sideways. I was terrorized as I didn't know the reason for having been picked out for this aggression. Many years later I came to the conclusion that it must have been as retribution for having been on the list of U.S. citizens. Block 19 stood out for the resistance it posed to forced labor and for the beatings it endured as a result: it was to become brutal, including dead and wounded. Tony Collado, my great friend and member of the Directorate, was impaled by a bayonet to the leg. He survived miraculously. Another prisoner, a member of the JOC called Chino Tan was not as lucky and bled to death from a bayonet wound at his assigned work site. Thus many others died due to conflicts during forced hard labor and many others got beaten because of the resistance we brought forth. Alberto Muller was taken to the Punishment Ward for arguing with a guard. I was also "condemned" to the punishment ward together with another fellow inmate and friend, Julio Hernández Rojo. We remained there for two months –from December to the end of February 1965– then we were returned to the building, this time sent to block 20. Mid–year, I was transferred again –this time to building 2.

La Cabaña Fortress

In May 1966 a massive transfer of 100 prisoners took place toward a prison at La Cabaña (galley 7), a fortress from colonial days at the entrance to Havana Harbor: I was among them. In the past, thousands of political prisoners had been shot to death there.

At La Cabaña there was no forced labor, and luckily I was among friends. Every night we would get together to talk and discuss books we had received or read. I recall that my aunt had sent me a book in French from New York. How come the guards did not censor it? Because President Charles De Gaulle was against the Vietnam War. I received "L'Apparition de l'Homme", written by Jesuit Priest Teilhard de Chardin. I read it with great gusto. It was about a scientific study about how man had evolved and developed through the centuries. I understood evolution to be heretical, as I had been taught in school. It became the source of deep questioning of my most deeply held beliefs. It was fascinating. I shared it with my friends and it lead to long discussions. At the time of his death in New York in 1955, Chardin's ideas were not accepted by the Catholic Church. But times change and today Pope Francis cites Chardin in his encyclical "Laudato Si".

$$= \circ = \circ = \circ =$$

Meanwhile, back in the prison at the Isle of Pines hard labor continued. Early 1967 we were told that there were plans to empty the prison in the Isle of Pines. Soon, transferred prisoners started arriving at La Cabaña from the Isle. Many of them were old friends of ours. We were kept in galley #7 while the new arrivals were spread out over the five remaining galleys.

Soon afterwards rumors began to circulate that the prison authorities were planning to change the yellowish uniform we had worn from the start for another blue in color, which was what common prisoners wore. Political prisoners like me considered this measure to be offensive as it mixed us up with the general population of ordinary prisoners. The purpose of the Cuban government was obvious: to be able to tell the world that in Cuba there were no political prisoners. Internationally, it was common knowledge that there were a huge number of prisoners suffering long sentences ordered by the Cuban government, a fact that had been brought up at international forums such as the UN. In 1965,

Castro had admitted that there were 15,000 political prisoners in Cuba.

Suddenly, one night the jailers selected a group of us drove us by bus from La Cabaña to the Castillo del Príncipe, also a colonial-era fortress. Traditionally this was the place where criminal court was held. The 50 prisoners taken there were separated into two large galleys where their yellowish uniforms were taken away from them, leaving behind on the floor a pile of blue ones and demanded to wear these instead. We did not comply with the order, therefore, remaining in our underwear – a new struggle was about to start.

The following morning, when the guards saw us in our underwear, they brought in common prisoners to the galleys where we were. To our surprise, these common prisoners respected us greatly. They sat down on the floor of the galley, away from us, "the political ones." Immediately we decided to go on a hunger strike. Ten days went by and we were still refusing food, only drinking water. Once again the guards took us out from the galleys where we had been and placed us in the adjoining ones.

It was the month of August, 1967. Castro was getting ready to host a great world assembly in Havana, which he labeled "The Tricontinental." The August weather in Cuba in August is very hot, at times asphyxiating. My fellow inmates and I –25 in all– slept on the floor. The wall of this galley was next to the jail bakery. It was always hot and humid from steam. The only way to bear the steam was to take a bath, but there was only one water faucet and we could collect water only with our food plates which we used to pour water over ourselves two or three times a day. Surprisingly, one day the guards took out two prisoners from our galley and we never saw them again. A few days later they took some others out – none were coming back. It was a mystery.

Still in my underwear, the guard took me to see my parents who had been allowed to visit me so as to convince me to wear the blue uniform. The visit lasted for half an hour. It was a very painful encounter, but I didn't give in. Then they transferred me to a different galley in that same colonial fortress. There, I met with other prisoners who had also refused to wear the blue uniform. There were but a few that accepted to change uniforms, and those were immediately sent to the farms of the Rehabilitation Plan.

The unruly like me were sent back to La Cabaña. We stayed there only a few days. The guards selected a different group —approximately 100 inmates including me— and pulled us into police cruisers with prisoner compartments, for a long journey without food or toilet to the Boniato Prison in Santiago de Cuba, at the other end of the island. There I was to share a cell with another 20 men sleeping on the floor. I remember that we would spend time playing Parcheesi and Monopoly, board games that we made ourselves. On June 6, 1968 the guard on duty gave us a newspaper where the assassination of Robert Kennedy was front page. One of my cellmates said he was glad because Kennedy was a Communist. I got very angry and condemned his absurd statement. We almost got into a fist fight, but thanks to the intervention of our cellmates the incident did not turn worse.

After a few months in these conditions, early 1968, the prison authorities at the Boniato prison decided to allow family visits again, always hoping that we would accept to wear the blue uniform. My parents had to make the long trip to get there, now clearly aging, to see me in such condition. Even so I did not accept to change into that uniform.

= o = o = o =

In July of that year we were transferred back to La Cabaña in Havana. Something very important had taken place in the high command of the Cuban government: the Minister of the Interior, the sinister Comandante Ramiro Valdés, who had been in charge of the internal security apparatus (including prisons) since the early days of the revolution was substituted by the also Comandante Sergio del Valle, a medical doctor who had also fought at the Sierra Maestra.

Sergio del Valle personally visited a galley of prisoners at La Cabaña to inform about new dispositions (I was still at the Boniato Prison in the Province of Oriente). He told the prisoners that we would be returning to the yellow uniforms (which we considered to be the ones of political prisoners). We were also to receive visits from our families and the food would improve. He even stayed around talking to the prisoners! He was asked what was going on in Czechoslovakia, the Prague Spring and Alexander Dubcek. His reply was: "The Czechs are doing what they have to do."

In a few more days they brought us back from Boniato. They allowed us to listen to the news and music. For the first time I heard the song "Let it Be" by The Beatles. I have always thought that this song is dedicated to the Virgin Mary (....."Mother Mary comes to me, speaking words of wisdom...."). Our Lady has always been with me: ever since she saved me from the firing squad, through the years of abuse and suffering and now in this new stage of my life.

After the Soviet invasion of Czechoslovakia, Fidel Castro took several days before uttering a comment. When he did, before a group of Party members to "orient them," we were able to listen to the whole thing by the prison's public announcement system. He began his comments saying: "in Czechoslovakia there has been a counter-revolution" – murmuring was heard throughout the room which Castro interrupted saying that he was going to explain very well what had happened. The official Cuban press had been publishing news stories about this daily, and of course Sergio del Valle had said that "the Czechs are doing what they have to do." At that point in time Castro had to justify the Soviet action in order to continue to receive their aid and remain in power.

= ○ = ○ = ○ =

Several days after trying on my new yellow uniform, a group of prisoners "considered it opportune" to launch into a hunger strike to demand more benefits. My fellow prisoners, those close to me in the struggle and others closely allied, did not accept this idea that did not seem opportune to us given recent developments. A few days later the guards opened all the gates of the galleys telling us that everyone who was not on strike was to exit the galleys. Several hundred men went out. They put us on buses headed to the Guanajay Prison, in a town west of Havana.

$$= \circ = \circ = \circ =$$

Guanajay

When we got to Guanajay we were told that our living conditions were going to change. The warden of the prison was Lieutenant Tejeda. During a recess at the prison courtyard the Lieutenant approached us to talk to us. He told us that going forward we would be able to come out into the courtyard to take in the sun and to practice sports if we so wished. They showed moviefilms once a week and there would be monthly family visits.

It is important to highlight that this was the year 1968 and several incredible things were going on. Not only the Soviet invasion of Czechoslovakia, but also the student rebellion in France (Paris) and in the U.S. (Berkeley, Columbia, etc); the Latin American Bishops Conference in Medellín, (Colombia), and the visit by Paul VI. And finally the horrific assassinations of the Reverend Martin Luther King and Robert Kennedy in the U.S. Our world was on fire.

We, the prisoners, got information that the armed struggle against Castro by the organizations we knew about was over. Only our families remained, suffering with us. It was necessary to find a dignified solution to imprisonment. For the first time the government was treating us as human beings. There were no further pressures on us. We organized basketball and baseball teams to compete among us. It was the year 1969 and living conditions in Guanajay remained as they were when we arrived.

It was then that Fidel Castro called for "the ten million sugar harvest." His goal was to achieve the production of 10 million tons of sugarcane in the 1970 harvest. It was to be the most important goal and to achieve it he dismantled the logistic chain of all other areas of production and services to mobilize a large part of the urban population to the fields. The goal was not reached and the country ended up completely disorganized. In order to hide the dismal political fiasco, Castro exaggerated the "theft" of some fishing boats and ordered the celebration of a "carnival" at Havana's seaside promenade, known as El Malecón, where rum was sold from tank trucks.

= ○ = ○ = ○ =

Our prison in Guanajay was visited by a Comandante from the Bureau of Prisons, Enio Leiva, who established a dialogue with a group of inmates. He asked us why we refused to accept the Rehabilitation Plan that the government had proposed. We explained our reasons and from there emerged the draft of a "Work Plan." These visits took place publicly on several occasions.

While this was going on, my father's health deteriorated after years of suffering he had gone through and caused him a heart attack. My family called the authorities in Guanajay to let me know. From Guanajay I was driven in a patrol car to my house. It was the first time I was able to return home after leaving Cuba to go to the University of Chicago ten years before. I was not able to recognize neither my neighborhood nor my house. Plants had grown, everything looked different, older. My parents still enjoyed the aid and comfort of Teresa, my beloved Chacha, my nanny and cook who lived with them. I was allowed to spend an hour with them. It was a very sad visit. At that point I was 30 years old and my sentence was to be 30 years –I had no hope of living free someday. The Cuban revolution had consolidated and it was not even a revolution. I was taken back to Guanajay that same night.

= o = o = o =

The Catholic Church

In 1969, the Catholic Bishops Conference of Cuba published an open letter in which they condemned the U.S. embargo against Cuba. Several Cuban bishops had been able to participate in the Conference of Latin American Bishops in Medellín, Colombia and had breathed the new winds that were blowing inside the worldwide Church after the Second Vatican Council.

In the decade of the 1960s the Catholic Church in Cuba had been reduced to a bare survival level due to limitations and a sophisticated repression by the Cuban government. The expulsion of priests, the nationalization of private schools, and discrimination against believers, in addition to the emigration of most practicing faithful, had decimated the evangelizing activity to a great extent.

Meanwhile in the universal Church, the Second Vatican Council ended in 1965 presenting to the world a new vision in the practice of the faith. I was able to read the final document , "The Church in the Modern World" , while in Guanajay. Relations between the Vatican and Eastern Europe –controlled by the Soviet Union –improved within the framework of ecumenism. For me and for many of my Catholic friends the vision on how to confront Communism was changing. The new circumstances regarding the more humane treatment in prisons allowed us to study and to open up our thinking to the new reality in Cuba and in the world.

= o = o = o =

The Progressive Plan

In 1971, I was called by surprise to the prison office, together with my partners Alberto Muller and Alfredo Sánchez Echavarría, to let us know that we would be getting a "special pass" that would allow us to visit our homes for 24 hours. It was an extraordinary opportunity for me and for my friends. A light was opening up in our dark horizon. At home, for my parents, this was a festivity. Many family members visited me –everyone thought this was but a preamble to our future liberation. In fact it was not to be. It would take another five years of waiting until September 8, 1976 when finally our dream became a reality. A few months later we were informed about the implementation of a new plan for us. It would be called "The Progressive Plan" consisting of working in planned building projects and occasional permissions to visit our homes. It would not involve classes on Marxism or mistreatment. We were asked who wanted to join in. Immediately a movie came to mind *Bridge Over the River Kwai* where a group of British prisoners of war during World War II built a railroad bridge for the Japanese Army in Burma. I accepted to work hoping it would lead to my freedom.

Soon the first group was assigned to work in the Porcine Plan to build pig pens. Although I did not know anything about this type of work I was able to meet a land surveyor who taught me how to use measurement instruments. Since I had studied mathematics and measurements in school, it was not difficult for me to learn the basics and I was named Chief of the Planning Commission! A year after starting to work I was granted my first pass to go home for 48 hours.

Several months went by; I would work during the day and spend the night at the Guanajay Prison. Then a large group of us prisoners were transferred to a rural area in the south of the Province of Havana located between the towns of Alquízar and San Antonio de Los Baños. Our job was to begin the construction of a high school. The new plan conceived by the Education Dept. required students were to work half a day in the fields and attend classes the other half.

My first mission as land surveyor/topographer was to measure the plot of land assigned for the building of the school and to mark the exact location where the foundation was to be laid. We would return at night to sleep in barracks where a head count would be taken each morning and evening. During the day we could walk about freely within the worksite. Several months later we were all rewarded with home passes. Now that I had 48 allotted hours I was able to walk around the neighborhood. I got the impression I was in a totally unknown place. Nothing and nobody seemed familiar. All the known neighbors had emigrated. In their place there were other families and in the corner some dorms had been built for medical school students. The School of Medicine of the University of Havana was now located in the campus of the former Sacred Heart School for girls which used to be run by the order of nuns of the Sacred Heart.

My father took me for a stroll down to a place where he would meet with his friends. It was called the American Club on Prado Street: it had a restaurant and a bar. My father had a 1959 VW beetle that he had kept in good working order thanks to a garage mechanic that was able to procure parts (don't ask how) and was good at fixing anything that came up. This was a miracle and a luxury at this point in time as the State would requisition for itself any private automobile it could get its hands on, especially those VWs. My poor father, old and frail, had been able handle the upkeep of that car, in addition to running the household and obtaining food during the worst of times, all the while awaiting my return.

My first incursions into the new Cuban reality

During one of my first "passes" I recall that some friends introduced me to a girl. I invited her to dinner and dance at the Hotel

Riviera, on the edge of the Malecón seawall in the Vedado neighborhood –a place very popular with young people. I was surprised when she suggested that we get there early so as to eat well, as good quality food would be gone before long. I was surprised at that because during my teenage years girls never talked about food. It was considered to be in poor taste. It also caught my attention that 23rd Street –a very busy traffic artery in Vedado– hardly had any traffic now. It was as if cars had evaporated.

We worked hard to be able to get a "pass" but we would never hear them a word about our freedom. Approximately after a year in the Work Brigade they transferred me to the Assembly Brigade, which was assigned exclusively to put together the various pre-fabricated sections that went into the construction of the schools: 1,000 sections in all, and then on to the following job. In this fashion we assembled 15 or 20 high schools in rural areas.

In early 1973 I met María Elena –my wife of 46 years– through Vicky Zaldivar, wife of one of my fellow inmates. Vicky was very much a matchmaker and she was of the opinion that prisoners did not get to meet good girls during their home passes. María Elena was very pretty, a Catholic like me, something that had cost her dearly having to suffer injustices by the hand of the Cuban government which intended on having everyone, especially young people, become professed atheists. The attraction was mutual. Ours was a romance by mail, and dating only during my leaves.

= o = o = o =

Lacking diplomatic relations between Cuba and the U.S., the U.S. Embassy in Cuba was entrusted to Switzerland. I was still on the list of American citizens which would normally be visited by it, and so an official from the Swiss Embassy was assigned to interview me. The rules of the Cuban government did not allow me to leave my job to visit the Embassy. In February 1974 I was temporarily transferred to La Cabaña and from there I was taken to State Security at Villa Marista –a frightful building. The following day I was interviewed by an official from the Swiss Embassy since, as I mentioned, I was on the list of U.S. citizens. It was to be a formality –not a big deal– he only wished to know how I was doing!

However, my return to La Cabaña on the evening of February 14, 1974 was dreary. An office employee was there to tell me that my father had died and that I would be taken to the wake the following day. And so it was. My mother, María Elena and other close friends were already at the funeral home. I was only given one hour to console my mother before being returned to prison. That was one of the worst nights of my life: having to suffer the loss of my father without a goodbye, and while in prison. To make matters worse, at midnight some young prisoners and juvenile delinquents started a violent fight among them. Then, former Comandante and former President of the Federation of University Students, Rolando Cubela, in prison too accused of attempting to kill Fidel Castro, entered the scene. He asked the mob to stop fighting on account of the fact that one of their fellow inmates had just lost his father that day. I will always be thankful to Rolando for such a humanitarian gesture.

= o = o = o =

The guard returned me to the work camp and I continued moving around the Province of Havana building schools in the countryside getting leaves every now and then. I felt very lonely, as my mother felt this way too.

By now I knew María Elena profoundly, I loved her very much. She had also shown a lot of love as well during our year and a half of courtship. I decided to ask her hand in matrimony. We both wanted to begin a family, to have children, and to start a new life. She accepted, which was proof of extraordinary courage given the circumstances in which we lived.

I had a good relationship with Monsignor Fernando Azcárate, Bishop of Havana, who at the time was serving as pastor in a parish downtown. I asked him to marry us and he accepted to go to the Corpus Christi Church on November 30, 1974 to officiate the wedding close to my home.

The prison office, for the first time, granted me a six-day leave in honor of the occasion. I had time for the wedding ceremony in the church that November 30, 1974, a reception at home and five days of honeymoon in Varadero Beach. It was a very happy time, unexpected and bittersweet. After this I went back to the school construction worksite as stipulated. The next leave would take place in December.

The New Year 1975 began with big news in January: María Elena was with child. The birth would be in September. My life was beginning to change dramatically. October 2nd, our first child, Ignacio Javier, was born. I was told about it at my worksite and they gave me three days off to go see him. When I arrived at the clinic where they were and I was able to see them both, my wife and I cried together a lot. Ignacio was a pretty and strong baby, and for this reason we lovingly nicknamed him "The Boxer." He was a gift from God which we accepted joyously. The new grandmas were also crying in joy.

= o = o = o =

Our life changed radically after the birth of our first child. We had something in common to fight for. The past appeared dead; the dictatorship seemed to have stabilized. The long-awaited day of being freed from prison was nearing as there were encouraging signs as some close friends had been let out already.

Finally, on September 8, 1976 a group of almost 20 prisoners –well-known Catholics– was summoned; the great day had arrived for us. Significantly, that is the day in which we celebrate the Patroness of Cuba, the Virgin of Charity of El Cobre.

Infinite joy abounded for my whole family when I got home. Little Ignacio was about to turn one year old. María Elena and I decided to celebrate in Varadero, the three of us. My parents had been able to save from confiscation a small apartment two blocks from the beach. Another one which they preferred had been confiscated long ago. At any rate, this one seemed like paradise to us. We got busy trying to get Ignacio used to the water at the beach; it took some doing to get him to enjoy it. To me it was like a dream to begin a new life, although the future was uncertain.

Back at the house I still had no job –I could sleep in and could take Ignacio for a stroll around the neighborhood, and little by little I was teaching him to walk. Towards the end of the year, the government passed the Anti-Vagrancy Law. People had to work or they would go to jail. My friend –and Ignacio's godfather– Ricardo Sarabasa, had friends in a government construction office. I applied for work, and since I had worked in construction I was taken –not as topographer but as planner. It was good that I was familiar with the "critical path." I was assigned to Teacher Trainers, consisting of three construction work crews. Block 18 was headed by Gerardo Colomé, who henceforth would be my boss. The place was not close by, but I had inherited my father's VW, and it was in good condition, as well as Felipe, his long-time mechanic.

The place where I ended up was Lenin Park on the outskirts of Havana. The site was huge; it had been mapped out by Celia Sánchez (Fidel Castro's intimate friend since Sierra Maestra days) conceived as an entertainment location for the general public, especially for children. Everything revolved around the magnificent Las Ruinas Restaurant, with its novel and artistic architecture featuring stained glass windows mounted on the walls of an old coffee plantation house; a work of art.

After so many years in prison, the experience of working with a construction crew made up of poor and humble Cubans that I had never met before – was a great experience. These were men and women who, overcoming all manner of difficulties, would show up to work hard under the sun for eight hours to then go back to the same difficulties to get back home. To them the benefits of the revolution were to have free healthcare and education, paid for by the government.

Our family life went on its course in 1976, we still had no idea that we would leave Cuba. María Elena had begun to work at the Embassy of France. The home now had two salaries.

We were able to visit Corpus Christi Church weekly and in so doing we were strengthening our faith and receiving solace from the Masses. This parish was run by a Canadian religious order. The priest could only come on Sundays but the nuns were very active in the religious training of parishioners. This is where we had been married and where we would baptize our two sons.

The church was near the former Havana Yacht Club, which coincidentally had been turned into a social club for construction workers, coincidentally. It had taken the name Julio Antonio Mella, the famous anti-Machado student leader of the 1930s. Sometimes we would go there after Mass for a bit of relaxation.

Now a bit more secure, we longed for our second child. María Elena was able to enjoy a more normal and peaceful pregnancy. David was born on December 3, 1977, very different physically and in temperament from his brother. He was a beautiful baby with big blue eyes that everyone admired. We thought he would be a girl because of his quiet and peaceful demeanor even before birth.

= o = o = o =

The armed struggle against the system had failed long since, and many had simply left the country in the belief the "there is no solution to this." The embargo decreed by the U.S. government on Cuba, of indefinite duration, was not working. It even contributed to people's resentment towards the United States, something the Cuban government took advantage of in its propaganda, diverting all blame to the U.S.

$$= \circ = \circ = \circ =$$

The University

In January 2018, I began to study Economics at the University of Havana. I was admitted on account that I was a construction worker and that my crew chief was backing me. We had a good relationship because I worked well and did not create problems for him. I only lasted six months in school. Economics required a lot of math, which I detested. However, in this short time I learned a lot about the college scene under the regime. The subject Marxist-Leninism was required on all majors. It was sort of a religion class called Marxism. On the first day the professor said that Marxism was very creative and that we had to discuss it openly as regards to conditions in Cuba. I recall that I asked an innocuous question. Nobody else asked anything, and in subsequent classes, the same, nobody asked anything. This went on until the end of the semester. It was an acquired and customary routine. The objective was to recite the material from the book to pass the class. Marxism was not creative at all: it was only a dead religion. Getting to talk to the students I realized that upon graduation I would be assigned to work in some state organism not of my choosing. Economists were technocrats of a system that obviously doesn't work and where everything that goes wrong is the fault of the U.S. embargo. I had already experienced this in the daily practice of preparing production statistics. The crew chief was only interested in achieving the assigned "goals" and in so doing he would alter the real figures with fake numbers.

The Dialogue

In November 1978, started the so-called "Dialogue with the Cuban Community Abroad", which allowed me to get in touch with very capable people with open minds. I believe that the Cuban government was not expecting the image projected by these visitors. They inspired respect in the population that met them, opening doors to the outside world. Among them I reencountered my old friend Father Oslé, who had been Director of the Cuban JOC (Catholic Workers Youth). I was introduced to María Cristina Herrera, who presided over the Institute of Cuban Studies in the U.S. Old friends from Belén School: Ricardo Puerta and Rolando Castañeda were members. The Institute was very peculiar. Its members were basically college professors interested in Cuban issues. We had a good relationship until her death. Another member was Reinol González, former member of the CTC, the Nat'l Union of Cuban Workers.

These happenings led to us to find out that all former political prisoners in Cuba were marked for life. Our IDs – which we used for everything – had a stamp, easily recognizable by the Police at any point. Reinol told me about this during the days of the Dialogue when he had futile talks on the matter with government authorities. This affected all former prisoners who were trying to lead a normal life as citizens of the country. This was unacceptable to me and to my family: we were second-class citizens.

= ○ = ○ = ○ =

As doors closed on us, the alternate path of leaving our nation in search of freedom became more feasible. My hope of living in Cuba despite having suffered prison for political reasons appeared to some to be a fantasy, especially to my family living abroad. María Elena had her whole family in Cuba and evidently it would be hard for her to abandon them. I was thinking about my sons and the future that awaited them, being as I was a marked man for life. In a chat with Monsignor Azcárate I was indecisive: he told me that he had been in the meeting of Latin American Bishops in Medellín in 1968, and based on its decisions, the Holy Spirit had illuminated him to propose to the other Cuban Bishops the need to hold a Council in Cuba. The idea of staying to help out seduced me, but in the end – and with María Elena's approval – we made the decision to leave Cuba. Years later, in 1986, Monsignor's idea became a reality with the celebration of the National Ecclesial Meeting of Cuba (ENEC), which was akin to a rebirth of the Cuban Church.

≡ ∘ ≡ ∘ ≡ ∘ ≡

Preparations for the Trip

In 1977, Jimmy Carter was elected President of the United States. Diplomatic relations between the two countries could be possible in a not so distant future. Interests Sections were reopened in Cuba and in the U.S. respectively; and the "Dialogue" had achieved permission by the Cuban government for Cuban Americans to visit the island. Family meetings brought joy to everyone involved opening a horizon to the world for the Cuban people.

The U.S. Interests Section in Havana contacted my mother and I, as both of us were on the list of American citizens stuck in Cuba, and they offered us help to be repatriated. The Cuban government, for its part, wanted to get rid of former political prisoners. Everything went well and three months later, on August 30, 1979, we were able to fly to Miami aboard an airplane chartered by the U.S. government to evacuate its citizens –although not before the State authorities had taken over our house, including the VW beetle car. Also left behind was Teresa (my Chacha) who had decided to remain behind to help out her family, and María Elena's family as well. The State provided an apartment for Teresa to move in as the house had to be vacated and made available to the government.

Arrival in Miami

We arrived at a terminal removed from the airport and after clearing Customs and being greeted by social welfare agents assigned to new arrivals we were taken by bus to Tropical Park to reunite with our family members. Waiting for us there were my cousins who took us to the house of my mother's cousin. This house was located at N.W. 25th Avenue near Miami Senior High School. During my childhood visits to Miami I used to spend several days there. At that time the neighborhood was typically American. In 1979, the neighborhood was known as Little Havana. Everything had changed.

On October 7, 1960 I had left alone from Miami bound for Havana and now 19 years later I was returning bringing with me my mother, my wife and my two sons, ages one and three. My second world had come to an end –a third one was beginning, filled with dreams, and thanking God for having allowed me to survive.

Personal photos

**REMAINS OF THE CIRCULAR PENITENTIARY
OF ISLA DE PINOS
WHERE I WAS KEPT IN PRISON FROM
FEBRUARY 5, 1961 TO MAY 1966**

WITH FRIEND ALBERTO MULLER

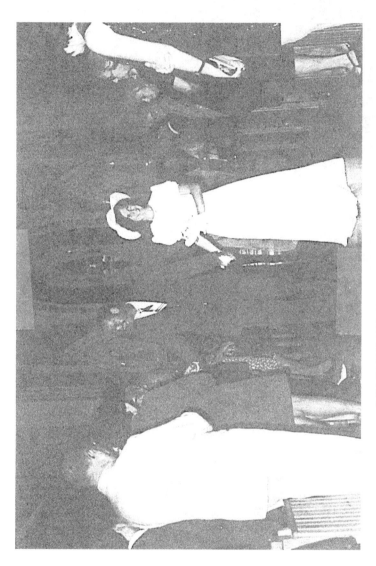

DAY OF OUR WEDDING NOVEMBER 30, 1974
CORPUS CHRISTI CHURCH, LA HABANA, CUBA

**MY WEDDING OFFICIATED BY
MONSEGNOR FERNANDO AZCARATE**

IN OUR HOME

IN OUR WEDDING DAY WITH MY BRIDE'S PARENTS,
JAIME MUXO AND DELIA ORTEGA
AND MY MOTHER CARMEN CREWS IN OUR HOME

VIRGIN OF CHARITY OF EL COBRE
I WAS RELEASED FROM PRISON
SEPTEMBER 8, 1976
DAY OF CHARITY OF EL COBRE

**WITH MY WIFE MARIA ELENA
IN VARADERO AFTER MY LIBERATION**

MY WIFE AND I IN CIENFUEGOS
(IN THE BACKGROUND EL CASTILLO DE JAGUA)

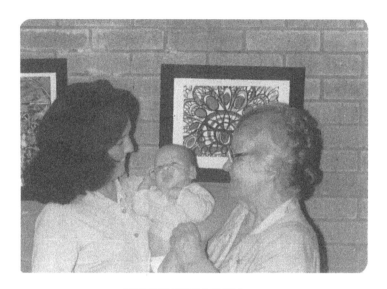

MY WIFE MARIA ELENA
AND MY MOTHER CARMEN CREWS
WITH OUR FIRST SON IGNACIO GARCIA

MY WIFE AND I
WITH OUR TWO SONS IGNACIO AND DAVID GARCIA
AT THE BEACH IN SANTA MARIA DEL MAR

WITH MY WIFE AND OUR TWO SONS BEFORE WE LEFT CUBA

THIRD WORLD

"God has told you, O mortal, what is good
And what does the Lord require of you
but to do justice and to love kindness
and to walk humbly with your God?"

(Micah 6:8)

THIRD WORLD

Our arrival in Miami on August 30, 1979 turned out to be a big celebration, especially for my mother's family. We had been a very close family, but by then her brother Joe had already passed away in 1956, and my grandpa Thomas Crews had also died in New York in 1967. My grandma Sofía Carrerá had died when I was a boy.

My cousin July and his three children welcomed us, as well as Gemma, cousin Eddy's wife, and my aunt Malala. My mom's cousin, Pat Crews Dowdell was away on vacation and so they let us stay at their house for three months. This was the very same house I had visited so many times during my visits to Miami before. It was located on N.W. 25th Avenue, very near to Flagler Street and Miami Senior High School. By 1960, the last time I had visited Miami before returning to Cuba to end up in prison, the city ended around 27th Avenue. When I got back to the U.S. for good in 1979, Miami had now extended to 127th Avenue. Today it reaches the Everglades. When I was a boy, the neighborhood was strictly "Anglo," but when I got back to "La Sagüesera" that is, the S.W. section of Miami, it had become populated by Cuban refugees that had settled there in the meantime.

The following day some old veteran fighters came by: Alberto Muller, Juan Manuel Salvat and Joaquín Pérez. It was a happy reunion filled with memories for all four of us. We had a good time with many other old friends. María Elena, for her part, was

115

saddened as she had left her family behind, so she set out to get to know mine better, and to take care of our two little treasures everyone would fuzz about, who would never tire from running and jumping around with their cousin Lolo. They felt something good was happening, although they didn't understand what it was. Then they discovered *Sesame Street,* which became a blessing for many years.

After the first days of euphoria and invitations, the adaptation to our new reality began for our lives in a new world. I was already 40 years old and with a family to feed. I understood that it would be hard to start again, late in life.

Our dear friend Lidia, who in Cuba had been my father's secretary for many years, had kept in touch regarding our needs in Cuba. My father had given her some money to take care of us back then, and now she gave us the rest of the money she had been holding. This allowed us to fend for ourselves for the first few days.

A few days after my dear cousin Eddie arrived from Venezuela –he was for me like my big brother who had tried unsuccessfully for so long to get me out of prison and out of Cuba. He was now the President of Bristol Meyers in Venezuela, and he did a lot of traveling. Our longed-for reencounter at the airport was indescribable for both of us. In 1960 I had sought refuge from the State Security in his home, always fearing that he would also get in trouble on my account, something that would have been an additional tragedy as he was newly married and his wife was with child in the midst of all these hellish times.

My family was very supportive as we were getting ready to start over. I, an eternally optimistic guy, was sure that God and his Blessed Mother would protect us as always in this situation, no matter how difficult it could get. After twenty years, I was no longer the only child of a well-to-do family. My father had lost all his properties and his business had been confiscated by the Cuban Government. Additionally, we had to vacate and hand over our house where we lived to the State in order to be allowed to leave. Now we were living in a big city (that's how it seemed to us). Many Cuban refugees had arrived at a time of economic boom in the nation and this had afforded them many opportunities which, accompanied by their drive and hard work had allowed them to make a good living. The first and greatest of these opportunities came with the *Cuban Adjustment Act of 1966* during the Lyndon Johnson Administration. Never again has a similar law been granted for refugees of other nationalities. However, many were not aware of this privilege. And Cubans have paid back the favor: before their arrival in the 1960s, Miami was a small Southern tourist town where African-Americans had to sit at the back of the bus while public schools were segregated as well as many other of the usual scourges found in Southern States. But by 1979 there were already several Cuban radio stations, restaurants, large enterprises, and all manner of small businesses, also in Cuban hands, and let's not forget many healthcare professionals.

In the Cuba I had left behind, there was the totalitarian Castro dictatorship led by one man who had swindled his people. The armed struggle against that system had ended and replaced instead by an incessant string of threats from abroad that were fuel for the regime's propaganda. Repression had been perfected to the highest degree. The Catholic Church, after being crushed during the early years, was just reawakening. It was the sole institution from the past that was still standing, although greatly scrutinized.

My old friends and comrades-in-arms who had arrived in the United States during those twenty years were by now very well-respected professionals or businessmen who were satisfied with their efforts. They all held a great love for Cuba and a deep sense of nostalgia for those bygone times. For me it was a time that called for a lot of work in seeking the path that I needed to follow.

That September 1979 I took a quick trip to Dubuque, Iowa, to visit my great friends, the Wahlert family. As usual, I was

117

warmly welcomed, this time by Bob Jr. and Dick Weber, my teenage friends. Bob Wahlert, Sr. had kept up with my father during my long years of confinement always helping him. Bobby, Jr. had married his girlfriend Donna – whom I had met back then – and had several children. Their welcome brought back many happy memories. Additionally, as my father had business dealings with Wahlert, he honestly saved the remaining monies and handed them over to me. I returned to Miami a bit more relieved, ready to think about the best use to give it. God and my father had already provided me the first assistance. With this money we settled down in Westchester, a nice community west of Miami.

One day, one of my friends took me to visit the *Agrupación Católica Universitaria*, still led by Father Llorente in Miami. It was on the other side of the city, on the east, by the sea. I got a nice welcome, but I got the impression that everything had changed since the days when I was jailed. It was no longer that vibrant place, full of young people, mainly college students, which I had joined when I was 18. Now it was mainly a retreat center. In Cuba we would celebrate Sunday mass at the *Agrupación* – but in the U.S. families go to their respective parishes, a much better idea. We selected Divine Providence, near our home.

My cousin Eddy invited me to spend a few days at his house in Caracas to check it out in case I wished to start my new life there. My good friend Joaquín Pérez also lived in that city. He had a beautiful family including many children. He invited me to go on a helicopter ride, so I saw many beautiful landscapes. The country enjoyed economic wellbeing, due to its oil bounty. But I also got to see the shantytowns on the slopes of the mountains that surround the city. These are the areas where the poor live, those that were not participating of the abundance. I thought right away that this was the perfect storm for a demagogue "Messiah" to come promising justice that would go unfulfilled. I had already lived through all that.

Ricardo Coronado, my friend from the Belén neighborhood in Havana, and a former classmate, lived in San Juan, Puerto Rico. I was also able to visit him, and for the first time I saw that island.

I came to the conclusion that the best place for my family to live, especially our children, was in the United States.... after all, I was an American citizen with a legal resident wife and children at that time.

In 1980, my cousin-in-law, Alfredo Estrada, offered me a job as his representative in Florida. His company was established in Houston. I accepted it and worked for him for six months. It was a great experience.

Since Real Estate is a main source of income in Florida, I decided to study to get a license as Realtor. Another great friend of mine since childhood at Belén, Eduardo Muñiz, had a land sale business in the Florida Gulf Coast. As my grandfather would say: "the most important thing in life are good friends." Eduardo took me to visit a land broker in Fort Lauderdale, International Preferred Enterprises. Incredibly, the owner, Donald Soldini, had been in the Sierra Maestra with Fidel Castro during his youth. He was still nostalgic about those years and enjoyed talking about Cuba and the Cubans. He had gone back to New York soon after the revolution was over.

Soldini also knew my friend María Cristina Herrera, founder of the Institute of Cuban Studies in Miami. María Cristina would hold sessions at her home in Coral Gables on social and political topics about the island. She would invite interesting people to talk about these topics. There, I met several U.S. university professors, experts in Cuba viewed from abroad, in full freedom and with new perspectives. The members of the Institute were not in agreement about restarting an armed struggle against Castro. They were rather interested in objective discussions about the Cuban reality. I was impressed and surprised that they were radically against the U.S. embargo on Cuba, something I agreed with after living the life of an average Cuban for three years after leaving

119

prison. I came to understand that the embargo was victimizing the people even more, giving Fidel Castro the opportunity to fault the U.S. for all the errors and abuses that the system had implemented. Additionally, it contributed to keep the people isolated and lacking news about the world outside, something that was perfectly suited to his purposes.

In the year 1981, Donald Soldini offered me the job of Sales Manager of his new land sale project. The land was mainly in Texas and the purchasers Mexican nationals. It was a generous offer and I accepted it, despite the fact that I had to travel most of the time. My family had to stay behind in charge of María Elena who had quickly found employment. I would spend six weeks in the Mexico/Texas area and two weeks resting back with the family. The two kids were growing up needing the presence of their father, but back in Miami I had not found any comparable job opportunity.

The President of Mexico in those days was López Portillo, called López el Pillo (rascal) on account of his corruption. In February, I arrived in Monterrey, a city known as a center of business and investments. From there I planned my operation in the rest of the country. I lived at the *Ancira Hotel*, famous for the incident when Pancho Villa entered its lobby mounted on a horse. I liked Monterrey. To begin with I placed ads in the newspaper in order to make contact with agents to sell land at Lago Vista and Horseshoe Bay, near Austin, Texas. Prospects would be flown to San Antonio and then taken in car to these lakes. It was not an easy job, and neither did I see myself working in sales, but my efforts brought about the income I was seeking. In general, I developed good relationships with Mexicans. I recall they told me I talked like *"Tres Patines"*, the famous Cuban comedian they knew from his legendary recorded radio show, very popular there.

I was always looking forward to my return to Miami, as was my family. We enjoyed it a lot. My mother continued to live with us, and the boys were growing up happily. In August we were able to afford a two-week vacation at Sanibel Island beach. I could not complain.

Meanwhile, in other places in the world other events were happening. Pope John Paul II, elected in 1978, visited Poland in 1979 and after his visit, a labor movement started: Solidarity, and its leader Lech Walesa. On the other hand, in Cuba in 1980 a mass exodus of discontented citizens against the regime took place. All in all, approximately 125,000 Cubans found their escape valve through the Port of Mariel, west of Havana. Their family members from Miami went to get them by boat. This meant a great change for Miami.

In 1982, a great financial crisis took hold in Mexico. The exchange rate changed from 24 to 48 and soon thereafter it plummeted to 72 pesos to the dollar. The purchase of land in the U.S. became too expensive for Mexicans. The project was doomed. Then, my boss, sent me to Venezuela. Soon the Venezuelan Bolívar went from 4 to 8 to the dollar overnight. I had to move on to Panama but business opportunities there were nil, but I was able to see Pope John Paul II during his visit to the stadium in the capital.

In Panama I caught fever and headaches as I had never experienced before. I had to get back to Miami in June 1983 and was diagnosed with Hepatitis A, ending up in the hospital.

Soon before being diagnosed with Hepatitis A I had a very important conversation with my parish priest, Father Patrick Flynn – a psychologist. Father Flynn was a family friend who was willing to do us a great favor: he met with my son Ignacio to analyze what we could do to help him after his diagnosis of hyperactivity due to Ignacio's incessant level of activity. This priest was very charismatic, and his homilies were usually very good. On one occasion I explained my feelings that I hated to be in sales; but how, thanks to this job, I had been able to feed my family. He told me that I was deeply depressed, which was absolutely the case. We held this conversation a few months before I contracted hepatitis. I had to stay at

121

American Hospital for 17 days, three of them in a coma. My life was in danger. Once again, God saved me and gave me another opportunity. The percentage of deaths in similar cases stood at 80%. The virus paralyzes and destroys the liver. The brain fills with toxicity, causing memory loss and difficulty in speaking. The heart has to be constantly monitored. I completely forgot the English language, although luckily my doctors were Cuban. Nobody, except María Elena, was allowed in my room for fear of contagion. Father Flynn would bring me the Eucharist.

Despite its seriousness, the disease does not leave behind permanent damage, and so, once recovered, my faculties returned to normal. I attribute my illness to a loss of my immunity due to depression. I have never had liver problems since.

Now I was back home without a job or savings, with a family to provide for on María Elena's salary only, which was not enough to pay the mortgage on the house where we lived. My complete rest was essential, and we had to spend several months under these conditions with the help of my family members. As there is no cloud without a silver lining, my spiritual life intensified considerably during this time. Someone in my parish gave me a recording by Father Richard Rohr (a young Franciscan), and Father Flynn gave me a lecture by monk Thomas Merton which I will never forget: "A devoted meditation about the memoirs of Adolf Eichman." Merton's meditation was fantastic. Eichman, the murderer of thousands of Jews, was diagnosed by a psychiatrist as mentally sane while a faithful servant of Nazism. This marked the beginning of my interest in Merton's ideas, which I have kept up with to the present day. I am a member of the International Society named after him, having attended two of its meetings. María Cristina was also a Merton spiritual "disciple," and I still hold a book she gave me *–The Intimate Merton–* published by Patrick Heart.

= o = o = o =

After my recovery, I reached the conclusion that my life needed a huge change. I returned to my college studies although I was not sure about what should my major be. Meanwhile, with the assistance of a friend I got a job at the publishing house McGraw-Hill/Dodge Reports. The job consisted in gathering information from the technical point of view from engineers and architects regarding buildings in progress. It was the type of job that allowed me to go to school at night. Through Professor Jorge Salazar, economist and Dean of the Economics Department, Florida International University, FIU accredited me with enough credits to earn an equivalent Bachelor of Economics after obtaining only 30 additional credits at FIU. And that is how I was finally able to graduate in June 1986.

Now the question became: What should I do to make a living doing something that will satisfy me so as not to be always suffering about my line of work? Our kids were already growing up and we had plans for them to also go to college. I had to discern all this, and although my vocation focused on Sociology and History, I decided that I needed to study something that would allow me a secure way to make a living. I chose to go to Law School. I was admitted to the University of Miami. I started my studies in September 1986 at the age of 46.

= o = o = o =

On the other hand, my spiritual life was flourishing, matured by the experience of having been close to death. After my struggle for the freedom of Cuba, and the huge suffering that resulted from it, I observed that the ideas and theology of Vatican Council II, were penetrating the Church with what soon would become known as "the emergent church" –a different worldview of the church to which I have belonged from birth to the present day: A vision based on a Risen Christ that walks among us and calls us to follow him to the Sea of Galilee. This longing is made manifest in priests, laypeople, men, and women. It is a deepening of the Mystical Body of Christ which unites us and transforms us.

Back to school and entering the world of work

I felt great about going back to school to continue my studies, which had been abruptly paused on account of the events in September 1960. Now I was much more mature and happy. I was able to dedicate more time to my children, giving them advice and setting the example, as well as to playing basketball and taking care of making María Elena and my mother happy. My job as a reporter for McGraw-Hill Dodge Reports was fairly easy, although not well remunerated, but it did provide me with time off. María Elena was also working, thus helping out with the upkeep of the household. She also instilled in the children a discipline for their studies which would be invaluable for their future. Finally, the day of my graduation from Florida International University arrived in May 1986, with a Bachelor's degree, majoring in Economics. After much discernment I made the decision to go on to Law School. The University of Miami accepted me and although it was very expensive, it had the upside of making it possible to stay in town and take care of my family. From the first day I realized that my English literacy was not at the level required for law school. This is a field that requires a high level of language proficiency, including fluency in reading and the comprehension of difficult texts, and excellent writing skills. In a word, it was conceived for native speakers. This has always been a challenge and, making matters worse, I was the oldest student in the class. I felt intimidated and out of context. I had to resign from my job at Dodge Reports because I could not keep up with my schoolwork in a reasonable time.

Ignacio started seventh grade at the Belen Preparatory School in Miami. And David was starting the fourth grade at a selective program in International Studies aiming to a Baccalaureate diploma later. Every morning I would take David and Yolanda

(Alberto Muller's daughter) to school near the University of Miami, and then I would go to classes that would extend for most of the day. Although difficult, the subjects were mostly interesting, and the curriculum had many optional subjects to select from. I liked Constitutional Law, International Law, and above all Immigration Law. In the second year I took the "Clinical Program" which gave me access to a summer at the offices of the Public Defender in Court. A great experience! But, on the other hand, in order to graduate the curriculum included Business Law, Contracts, etc., areas that I did not like.

I was able to overcome my weaknesses and graduated in three years, as planned, in June 1989. Now I had to pass the terrible test to get my license ("The Bar") to practice in Florida. This meant a huge struggle for me for a long time. Still studying and with creditors demanding payment for my student loans I began to work for a law firm that specialized exclusively on Labor Compensation law. For me there was no doubt in my mind that my great dream was to practice Immigration Law, as it combined my vocation for social justice and my vision about international politics. In those years the liberation of Eastern Europe from the Soviet yoke was at hand. The Berlin Wall had fallen in 1989. The Soviet Union was in crisis, as was the Cuban government. My mission in the midst of this panorama was to pass the Bar and get a job to sustain my family and help others. By this time, nothing could deviate me from my goal.

After a second unsuccessful try at passing the Bar in 1990, my friend Luis Pérez talked to me about a possible employment opportunity at the Rural Law Center of Apopka – a small city close to Orlando. It was a help center for poor immigrants, mostly Mexican. The legal aid section was part of a set of social-economic assistance measures for families in crisis. It was led by three Notre Dame Catholic nuns, with the aid of the Diocese of Orlando, grants by the State of Florida, and donations from benefactors.

All of it fulfilled my aspirations at the time, except for an important detail: my family was living happily in Miami, and the kids were in good schools. Nobody wanted to move away from there. I would have to move alone to Orlando, living in a rented room during the week to go home on Fridays for the weekend. I spent a year doing this. I gained some experience about the life of suffering of immigrants and refugees, but to all practical purposes, I was a Paralegal as long as I had not passed the Bar. These were tough times that I would not be able to overcome for a long time.

Also employed at the Center was Father Mariano Cobas, a Colombian who served as spiritual guide. A real-life saint. He helped me a lot. His slogan was: "those who do not live to serve are not worth living." What an example he was to me in lending me a hand so I could move forward in my struggles! Soon thereafter he develped cancer and died on June 28, 1993.

Traveling back and forth between Orlando and Miami did not allow me to pass the Bar during the scheduled exams during those months. I could not go on like this. I realized we all needed to live together in Orlando in order to have a more normal life and not waste time. And so we did on October 31, 1991, as soon as we were able to sell the house in Miami in the middle of a market crisis. We left Ignacio in Miami for approximately one more year at the Hidalgo's home and later at the Zaldivar's. They were like brothers to us and their kids also attended Belen Jesuit. All this effort so he could graduate from his beloved high school.

David remained with us and started ninth grade at Bishop Moore High School in the Diocese of Orlando. This was the most painful episode for my family.

Leaving Miami

To describe what it meant for us to leave Miami behind – after 12 years – is hard to express. For me it left a sweet and sour taste. I had spent a whole year going back and forth every weekend. In that regard this was a relief. For the family the loss was greater. In Miami we had old friendships and family members. The kids were happy in their schools.

If leaving Ignacio behind was painful, what happened next was equally hard. My mother was already presenting symptoms of Alzheimer's in Miami. The change made it worse. She could no longer stay at home alone while we were working and conditions for the care of the elderly at home was almost inexistent in Orlando. Three months after the move, I had to place her in a Catholic nursing home with the help of our friend, Sister Lucy. This broke my heart. Five years later she passed away.

The City of Altamonte Springs, a few miles north of downtown Orlando, seemed ideal to me for our children to grow up and so we set roots there up to the present time. We were able to meet good friends such as Miguel and Carmencita García, which were by our side those first few difficult years. Our parish nearby offered us new acquaintances, different perspectives and nationalities.

A dream comes true

Finally, I was able to pass the Bar and was able to practice law in Florida. My swearing-in was in September 1992 at the Appeals Court west of Miami.

The joy and sense of relief that the whole family felt were unspeakable. I would be able to open my small one-room legal office, and of course, just as I had dreamed from the start, I specialized exclusively in cases related with foreign immigration into the United States.

The office opened November 1, 1992. We could not hold an open house because we had no money for it. This journey had left us high and dry, we had to pay back my student loans; yet we were full of expectations and plans for the future. My wife, as usual, was ready to help out, in addition to her fulltime job at the

Orlando Diocese, thanks to Sister Lucy Vásquez, a classmate and friend since childhood. She worked there for 17 years until her retirement in 2009.

My work at the Rural Law Center had provided me the opportunity to learn something about my area of work, and so I knew that there were migrant communities in the outskirts of Orlando. There were also many refugees from Latin America anxious to obtain political asylum and someone who could understand Spanish to help them.

= ० = ० = ० =

A Father's Pride

The year 1993 was a good year for my son Ignacio: he won the State of Florida's pole vaulting championship within his age group, graduated from Belen Preparatory School (Miami) and was admitted at Florida State University (FSU).

Two years later, David graduated with honors from Bishop Moore High School (Orlando), and was likewise admitted to college.

My children continued the tradition of their father as both ended up becoming attorneys, although neither in Orlando or Immigration Law. They graduated from Florida State University and Georgetown University, respectively, separated by a few years. Both passed the Bar quickly upon the first try. What a difference as compared to my odyssey, and what peace of mind this brought to us! I came to the conclusion that my struggles and the goals I had achieved had been a good example and a positive influence for them.

= ० = ० = ० =

John Paul II's visit to Cuba

Diplomatic relations between the Vatican and the Cuban government improved a bit. Fidel Castro invited Pope John Paul II to visit Cuba in January 1998. After 41 years of trying to eliminate the Church as an institution in our country, submitting it to harassment and discrimination against practicing Catholics, expelling priests, and nationalizing schools, new phase was opening up.

The visit by John Paul was monumental. The welcome that the people in general gave him seemed incredible. Many among the young born and educated during the Revolution could not figure out what was happening. My wife María Elena, who for 20 years suffered personally the consequences of remaining faithful to her beliefs, wanted to offer solidarity to the suffering Cuban Church, joining a group of Cuban American Catholics in celebrating such a grandiose event. They traveled from Tampa on January 20, 1998 to attend John Paul's Mass at Revolution Square on the 25th. There was an image of the Sacred Heart in the background. After his return from Cuba, the media asked the Pope what he felt when he saw the Sacred Heart presiding over Revolution Square together with Camilo Cienfuegos and Che Guevara. Paraphrasing it, as I do not have his words verbatim, the Holy Father said that it was not really out of place as, in the end, Jesus was the only one fomenting a real revolution.

I did not dare to go to Cuba at that time, but probably I would not have obtained permission to enter the country. I stayed behind helping Tennessee's Catholic TV channel to translate and explain the significance of this event.

In fact, starting in 1998, the harassment against the Church was substantially reduced, allowing it to expand its evangelizing work among the population.

= o = o = o =

Other events

The hard days since our arrival in Orlando were now part of the past. My profession was doing well. The AILA (American Immigration Lawyers Association) of which I am a member, kept me abreast of the frequent changes in Immigration Law.

In 1999 we were able to take our first trip together to Europe. It was a brief and modest one. María Elena selected Paris. This had been her dream since the days she worked at the French Embassy in Havana, and additionally, she spoke the language fluently.

In August 2001, we took David to Washington, D.C. as he was moving there to begin Law School at Georgetown University. There he was during the terrorist attack to the Twin Towers in New York and to the Pentagon in D.C. He underwent the worst day of his life. Someday he may be interested in writing about his experience. I, for my part, can relate mine: anguish, anger and sadness. Three years later, after graduating with honors and a job in New York, he decided to remain in Washington permanently.

Ignacio, for his part, had been a lawyer since 2000, settling down in Tampa with a good job. In 2003 he gave us the great joy of marrying Kristin, who would be a good wife and mother. They have given us three grandchildren: Jake, Tyler and Wesley. In June 2010, David married Magaly, born in Washington to Bolivian parents –an excellent girl– and they gave us two others: Lucienne and Matías. We gained two pretty daughters-in-law and five precious grandchildren. How many blessings!

In 2002, the Institute of Cuban Studies in Miami organized an event to celebrate the Centennial of the Republic of Cuba at the "Félix Varela Center" at the Shrine of Our Lady of Charity, our patron saint. I was part of a panel, and my paper was "The History of Violence in Republican Cuba." I divided it into three parts, taking a cue from French writer René Girard about the role of the "scapegoat" as it relates to the Jewish people narrated in the Scriptures. Several personalities and researchers of Cuban issues presented their work, and compiled them in a book which I still have. It was a great gathering for Cuban exiles.

= o = o = o =

President Obama

On January 20, 2009, David got a hold of tickets to attend Obama's inauguration as President at the Capitol steps. The crowd was estimated at more than a million people despite the cold wave battering the city. Many people were not able to go in – including us. The section assigned to our tickets did not get to open for the guests. We had to take comfort in listening to the speech from the outside together with many other unfortunate people. At any rate, we were able to see people crying out of happiness. For the first time we had elected an African American president. It was a historical moment that we enjoyed tremendously.

Pope Francis – his impact on my life

On March 13, 2013, a Cardinal from Argentina, Jorge Bergolio, was elected successor of Pope Benedict. When I heard the news, his Italian last name made me think they had elected another Italian as Pope. Later I found out he was born to an Italian immigrant family. He was the first Latin American pope, and a Jesuit at that. Additionally, he chose the name Francis, the founder of the Franciscan Order. At first, I could not believe it. In the past there had been some friction between Jesuits and Franciscans in Cuba because they had taken opposite sides in the Spanish Civil War. The new Pope, obviously, wanted to patch up past differences.

Soon, his priorities started to become evident. In his first trip outside of Rome he went to the island of Lampedusa, in southern Italy. There, he celebrated Mass with recently arrived refugees from Africa. His homily was a prayer for understanding regarding their situation and respect for human dignity. He condemned what he called "the globalization of indifference" towards your neighbor's pain.

During his first interview –which he granted to Father Antonio Spadaro, editor of the Jesuit journal *La Civiltà Cattolica* – the new Pope made clear that Vatican Council II was irrevocable, and that he wanted a poor church, for the poor. His Papacy would mark a change of course for the Church. In this way he would open new pathways for the universal Church.

The Jesuit Order has never extended to the Orlando Diocese (East-Central Florida). Therefore, after the election of Jorge Bergolio S.J. to the Papacy and his identification with Saint Francis of Assisi, I started to visit San Pedro Spiritual Center, run by Franciscan Friars. I had already visited there for retreats and Franciscan spiritual courses. With the passage of time, I joined the Third Order Franciscans. I always felt inspired by the example of Saint Francis. We used to discuss it during Church Social Doctrine classes at school: "Lord, make me an instrument of your peace." Today, I believe that non-violent resistance is the only possible path for reconciliation among human beings. Thomas Merton always insisted on this reality.

The opportunity came up to visit Italy as part of a group made up mainly by people from the capital. The flight Washington-Paris-Rome was long. Our guide welcomed us at the airport in Rome and took us directly to Assisi, to the convent where we would be lodged. A few days later we went to Rome. Finally, we were able to see Pope Francis during his weekly Wednesday audience. It was a moving and unforgettable experience.

= ○ = ○ = ○ =

My first trip to Cuba

In 2014, I decided to join my wife María Elena for the first time in her annual trip to visit her family in Havana, as well as to visit my cousin Enrique Don. David, our youngest son wanted to go with us. I felt I had experienced a spiritual transformation that allowed me to re-live many events for the first time after 35 years. As a

Christian I professed to be, I had to ascertain up to what point I had learned to forgive those guilty of so much human suffering levied upon my parents and me and upon the average Cuban citizen that had stayed behind. It was my way of coping with the memories and going forward. I did not wish to remain harboring old resentments, nor feelings of vengeance. However, I did not wish to forgive an absolutely totalitarian and economically inefficient system, whose few successes do not justify the abuse at the root of the material and spiritual misery of the Cuban people.

The Cuban Government had stripped away my father's business and properties, but thank God they left him alone, at home to live with his sorrow. Finally, he died February 14, 1974, victim of heart disease and diabetes. My mother was at his side all the time, and later was able to come and live with us in the United States, enjoying her grandchildren and the rest of her family until she died of Alzheimer's on January 23, 1997. Her last coherent words were: "I love Jesus with all my heart, and I want to see Him soon." The one person who first taught me to pray to the Sacred Heart of Jesus before going to bed every night returned home to the Lord.

In Havana, I wanted to re-live and tell my son about the place he was born, which we sadly had to abandon due to circumstances outside our control. I became very emotional watching its very bright blue sky which I had by now forgotten. I started out visiting the old neighborhood of Belén, where I grew up. I was able to visit my home and to sit for a while in my own room. Two blocks away from my home was Belén, my beloved school which had had a lot to do with my formation. Now the Government had turned it into the ITM, Military Technical Institute. My son commented that it looked more like a university. The guards did not even allow us to take photos of the building façade, but I had a good recall of the place, so I decided to turn around the corner and from that side I was able to take photos. We went by the small Trufín Park where I played when I was very young. We reached the gate of Tropicana, the best-known night club in Cuba and abroad. During the 1950s entertainers like Frank Sinatra and Nat King Cole performed there. The Cuban Government has dedicated the place only for tourists whom they drive there by bus from their hotels, so the building has been well preserved and is a great source of dollars. We were allowed to see it from the outside, and since it was daytime, to have lunch in the cafeteria.

Next, we drove by *"Ciudad Libertad"*, an educational complex housed in the former Columbia military garrison, from where President Batista fled Cuba, and where Fidel Castro ended his triumphal caravane all the way across the island in 1959. There, he gave a long speech full of unfulfilled promises.

After visiting my childhood neighborhood, we drove to my teenage neighborhood, the last place where I lived before leaving Cuba: the former Country Club, renamed by the revolution "Cubanacán". David was born there in 1977 and he was very excited to see his home again. The house and the empty lots around it had been turned into a vegetable laboratory by the Ministry of Agriculture. There was lettuce planted everywhere. We knocked at the door –noticing immediately that the garden in the front had disappeared– and we asked permission to go inside, explaining our reason. The answer was NO, we could only walk around the outside. We did, but we were able to sneak in through the back and see a bit more: the children's room (but not ours). David was delighted. Some commotion went on among the employees and they showed up. While I was taking a photo of them at the front door, one of them discretely told us: "Only in a photo am I able leave Cuba."

The neighborhood's appearance had changed a lot. The Sacred Heart nun's school is now the basic school for medical students, while most of the large mansions had been turned into foreign embassies. Only the palm trees of the Grand Boulevard remained as witnesses of bygone days. We drove down to the sea along the Boulevard and visited Corpus Christi Catholic Church, where we married and baptized our children. It was deteriorated, but still standing with the help of the Cuban Church.

Another important visit was to Old Havana, a place of contrasts. There we saw, on one side, the restoration work done by the Office of the City Historian: museums, restaurants, etc., while on the other side there were rundown and almost fully destroyed old structures where the average Cuban lives.

We took a stroll along the Malecón seawall –which will forever be Havana's waterfront promenade– full of nostalgic memories. From there, I pointed out to my son La Cabaña, a Spanish fortress that guarded the Port of Havana during colonial days. Today it is a museum dedicated to its early history, including the 9 p.m. cannonade salvo... and that was it. Nothing else is mentioned. The dungeons, the high walls often used by the firing squads during the first years of the Revolution, all the human suffering that was experienced behind those walls where I was imprisoned for years on end. NOTHING.

From Cuba I brought back a film made by the ICAIC (Cuban Institute of Cinematographic Art and Industry). The ICAIC was established at the beginning of the revolution and placed under the guidance of Alfredo Guevara, a well-known revolutionary and lover of the "seventh art." Of course, right off the bat its films got the strong backing of the revolution and some even won prestigious international film awards. But as the years wore on, facts could not be hidden for too long. Some films were considered controversial by the regime and withdrawn as soon as they were shown in the city theaters. This was the outcome for many, including *Regreso a Itaca,* script was written by the internationally famous writer Leonardo Padura. I was able to get my hands on a copy in the black market, not realizing how much it would make me reflect on all this.

The film is about a reunion of old friends in a roof-top shack overlooking the Malecón, improvised by one of them as his home. They were celebrating the return visit of a former group member who was residing in Spain after fleeing Cuba in frustrating, reprochable, and suspicious circumstances –as far as his friends were concerned– leaving behind a wife and son as well as his "revolutionary" ideals. All the characters were archetypical of Cuba's population, born and raised after Castro's Revolution. The film's musical score was the well known song back then, *"Ana María se fue con su bikini de rayas"*. The film was a reflection of the mentality in Cuba after decades of totalitarian dictatorship and the everyday life ideology. One of the characters concluded: "We wanted to change the world, yet the world has changed us." The painter in the group sadly recalled: "they kicked me out of the Communist Youth because I listened to the Beatles songs, and now it turns out that they built a statue of John Lennon for a museum in Old Havana." His frustration was due to the difficult life they were living, which included senseless personal and collective sacrifice. It was all an absurdity. Each of the five characters explained the sad reality of daily life in the country of their birth and formation. All this told in the street language of today's generation in Cuba.

= ○ = ○ = ○ =

Pope Francis' Visit

By the time we returned to the States, people were already talking about the timing of Pope Francis' visit to Cuba and the U.S. Finally, it happened in September 2015. We all sheltered great expectations about a Latin American Pope who spoke Spanish.

In Cuba, the meeting with young people at the door of Havana's Cathedral seemed to me the highlight of the trip although many young Catholics were unable to be in the area closest to the Pope. I don't think this was by chance. Despite it all, the speech given by the chosen young Catholic speaker representing them all in welcoming the Pope, was especially revealing. During his visit the Pope served as an intermediary in negotiations to restore diplomatic relations between Cuba and the U.S., broken off since

January 1961. For many reasons I considered this to be good news.

After Cuba, Francis flew directly to the U.S. where he enjoyed and enthusiastic welcome. Unfortunately, he didn't come to Florida as he went directly to Washington, D.C. to talk to a joint session of Congress. His best moment was when he mentioned four great citizens of this country: Abraham Lincoln and the Rev. Dr. Martin Luther King, Jr., as one can imagine, as well as Thomas Merton and Dorothy Day, two Catholics unknown to many in the audience. For me, of these last two the most important and exciting was Merton. The Pope described him "as above all a man of prayer, an inquisitive mind that challenged the conventional wisdom of the day, opening new horizons for our souls and for the Church. He was also a man of dialogue, a promoter of peace among peoples and religions." In June of that year, I had attended with several friends the annual meeting of the Thomas Merton International Society, which took place at Sacred Heart University in Connecticut. We established contact with several experts in the matter who offered us a wide vision of Merton and his work, as well as laying the groundwork for a future meeting.

$$= \circ = \circ = \circ =$$

Reestablishment of Diplomatic Relations

After the negotiations by Barack Obama to reestablish diplomatic relations with Cuba, I was convinced that the excuse used by the Cuban Government to justify its inefficient and abusive system had been eliminated: U.S. imperialist aggression. It was a fallacy that had been repeated for decades in an effort to turn it into a credible "truth," when in fact we all knew that the U.S. policy had changed a long time ago.

The Cuban people saw the heavens open up, considering the possibility to improve its precarious situation. The joy was palpable in the streets, the re-birth of hope. A poll taken at the time showed that the most popular figures in Cuba were Pope Francis and Barack Obama. Even "Panfilo", a folkloric comedian invited Obama to his TV show.

Obama's farewell at the National Theater in Havana –in the presence of Raúl Castro and the *"crème de la crème"* of Castro's hierarchy– was simply fantastic: Obama destroyed the myth of the victim and the aggressor, used by the Cuban government for decades, when he stated to Raúl Castro –in person and in front of the audience and the TV cameras– not to be afraid of the Cuban people.

Year 2016

This year started with great disappointment: Donald Trump was elected President of the United States thanks to the Electoral College. He had obtained 3 million less popular votes than his competitor, Hilary Clinton, but the EC count did not match that reality. During his campaign Trump declared that Mexican immigrants were murderers, rapists, and thieves.... while some were perhaps good, he said; and that he was going to build a wall to keep them out. Thus, he established a deep anti-immigrant precedent that would cause great pain and death in the future. As an immigration lawyer, a long struggle awaited me just to comply with the existing Law at the time.

Times change and so do politics

After his inauguration in January 2017, Donald Trump wasted no time in implementing his plans for the Mexican border. Television images showed the mistreatment and jailing of whole families and even the separation from their children who were placed alone in fenced cages. They were treated as criminals without consideration of evidence. There were unnecessary deaths which became a worldwide scandal. The exemplary work of charitable organizations and human rights defenders were widely published. It seemed impossible that such a situation could take place in the U.S.A.

Due to my profession, I knew the type of victim well. They are the ones who perform the work our own workforce discards with contempt: they work in farms where produce is harvested, as well as in meat processing plants of all kinds, while others build or fix roofs, or mow our lawns. Most of the time their wages are miserable, lacking benefits such as health or workplace insurance. All due to their illegal situation with very few resources for relief. They flee abuse and find rejection here. Despite this they are very productive, and educate their children to become good citizens even as they are threatened with deportation.

The Pedro Arrupe Jesuit Institute of Miami gave María Elena and me the opportunity to listen to and share ideas and activities in favor of this cause. My old friend and veteran of the struggle, Tony Sowers encouraged us with their plans, and we became members, despite the geographical distance.

= ○ = ○ = ○ =

Summer of 2017

I attended with María Elena the annual meeting of the Thomas Merton International Society at the Bonaventure Franciscan University, not far from Buffalo, north of New York State. There were almost 300 people there coming from throughout the U.S. and abroad. Priests and lay speakers were first class, as always. Once again, I was able to realize the influence Merton's thinking still exerts worldwide. Within the college campus there is a grotto housing a statue of Saint Theresa of Lisieux. The purpose of showing it is because Merton used to pray there daily. The story goes one day he heard sounds like bells from the Gethsemani Monastery (in Kentucky). This meant a call for him. He said farewell to his spiritual father at the university and soon thereafter, on December 10, 1941, he became a monk in Gethsemani where he remained for 27 years until his death on the very same day while he participated as speaker at a conference being held in Bangkok.

2018

Coinciding with the 50th anniversary of Thomas Merton's death, my friend Joaquín Pérez, President of the Pedro Arrupe Institute, together with Alfredo and Margarita Romagosa, organized a conference in which we recalled many important aspects of Merton's life and work, a spiritual explorer, as Pope Francis called him once.

In 2019, I could read *Catholicism and Citizenship,* written by Prof. Massimo Faggioli, where he explained how many of the developments agreed upon at Vatican Council II have not been implemented in the U.S., especially the document *Gaudium et Spes,* The Church in the Modern World. This made me think long and hard.

Stormy times

As time went by President Donald Trump's attitude towards immigrants increased and worsened. The promise to build a wall at the Mexican border and make Mexico pay for it was not achieved. But the cruelty against those waiting indefinitely inside and outside the U.S. to get the opportunity to be heard did. The illegal entry of entire families was criminalized and even small children were separated from their parents and placed in holding pens. Faced with a world-class scandal, the Trump Administration desisted from this policy although a few minors still remain housed in processing centers for various reasons. Meanwhile, the DACA program has been facing dismantling so as to deport youths brought by their parents before age sixteen – at times so young that ours is the only country they know.

After 25 years advocating for refugees and immigrants in general, I got to meet Father Alfredo Ortiz, parish priest of Misión Católica in Pierson, Central Florida, an area populated mainly by Mexican and Central American field workers who collect all sorts of vegetables, take care of plant nurseries, or cut lawns. Father Alfredo has invited me several times to go explain to his congregation, after Sunday Mass, about those immigration laws that affect them and the possible solutions that still exist, although with many limitations. An example of this is the case of José and Amelia, faithful members of the community for many years and adoptive parents of Juanito, a Mexican child who suffers from Down Syndrome, and whose father had been deported years before. The parents had left the child under the care of José and Amelia. I was able to get the Immigration Court Judge to hear his case, take pity on him, and grant him permanent U.S. residency status. The whole community celebrated the good news, really more like a miracle – and I was happy to have been able to solve such a humane and sad case. It gives meaning to my life as a Christian.

= ○ = ○ = ○ =

Our visits to Miami increased with time and our commitment to the Pedro Arrupe Jesuit Institute (IJPA). Early in 2019 – commemorating the 50th year of Merton's death— Alfredo Romagosa and I organized a presentation of his life. We had a good audience.

At the end of his famous first book *The Seven Storey Mountain*, Merton wrote: "this book ended, but the search continues." Merton was a spiritual explorer –and this is why I have been very motivated about his work for years in the U.S. Merton taught me about an unknown world from a new perspective for me. While in prison in Cuba, I had not had the opportunity of even knowing about his work. Years later I was able to read about his unhappiness and criticism of the Vietnam War, his defense of Rev. Dr.

Martin Luther King, Jr. in support of the civil rights of African Americans. I felt I was in the same wave.

= ∘ = ∘ = ∘ =

The **Arrupe Institute** has been dedicated to the defense and propagation of the theology of Pope Francis. We would read intently all his writings. In the Jesuit journal *America,* an ad appeared about a meeting "Following Pope Francis" at Villanova Catholic University in Pennsylvania (April 2019). Three members of the Institute decided to participate: Joaquín Pérez, President of IJPA; Sixto García, Theologian and retired Professor of Boynton Beach Seminary in Florida, and I. This meeting was attended by about 200 people from all over the country. Its presentations were very educational regarding issues and perspectives from the Pope. The introduction was given to **Cardenal Tobin**, from Newark, New Jersey. **Antonio Spadaro**, Director of the journal *La Civiltà Cattolica* who accompanies the Holy Father during all his trips, was in charge of the closing remarks. He mentioned that the ministry of the Pope can be explained using the phrase the of Spanish poet Antonio Machado: "Traveler, there is no ready-made road, you make it as you go" which was popularized by Catalonian singer Joan Manuel Serrat.

Repercussion in Miami

Our participation in the event "Following Pope Francis" was a stimulus for the Arrupe Institute. We decided to organize a similar event in Miami. **Alfredo & Margarita Romagosa, Tony Sowers** and others joined in. The Manresa Ignatian Spirituality Center assisted us by allowing the use of their premises in Miami for the Arrupe Institute activities. We started to prepare a bilingual program to which we would invite lecturers. The geographical position of the City of Miami is a natural link between Latin America and North America, and we wished to establish a bridge of ideas between the two cultures. With a huge effort from Joaquín Pérez and the Romagosas the first conference was scheduled for November 2019 with prestigious speakers from both worlds, all of them totally committed to the ideals of Pope Francis:

Sixto García, retired Theology Professor at the Diocesan Seminary of Florida, made the opening remarks explaining our objectives. **Thomas Massaro, S.J.,** Professor at Fordham University, New York, a prolific writer of the Church's Social Doctrine, shed light on the legacy of Pedro Arrupe, S.J.; and **Massimo Faggioli,** Professor at Villanova University and author of "Catholicism and Citizenship" provided an important contribution to the topics at hand. Prof. Rodrigo Guerra, Ph.D., commented on the Pope in *Aparecida;* Theology Doctor Carlos Schickendantz talked about how Vatican Council II was received in Latin America. The last two, from Mexico and Chile respectively, made their presentations in Spanish.

It became evident that in the U.S. there is a certain amount of resistance to the conclusions of the Council –especially to the document *Gaudium et Spes* – and as a result, to Pope Francis' implementation of it.

My small contribution

My fellow members of the Institute asked me to prepare a paper about immigration to the United States. This was a big challenge for me as I am not a professor nor a public speaker, but I accepted and enthusiastically thanked them for the invitation. I worked for months to write my paper, which included a slide presentation of the material. I called it "Globalization, Migration, and Social Justice."

Evidently, some aspects of globalization have to do with evangelization for Christians. Jesus told his apostles: "Go throughout the world and preach the Gospel." The Papacy of Francis makes a point of this during his visit to Lampedusa, where he coined the phrase "The Globalization of Indifference." John Paul II, in 1998, had supported "The Globalization of Solidarity" during his trip to Mexico where he named the Virgin of Guadalupe as Patroness of the Americas.

In the section about Immigration, I remarked that, although President Trump said the refugees from Mexico were rapists, thieves, and criminals, I have been able to ascertain that the majority of them are workers, escaping an unsustainable socio-economic situation that victimizes them. I compared this to the Exodus of the Israelites from Egypt to the Promised Land – and as closing, I mentioned the exodus of the Cuban people who escape from a totalitarian regime. Of this I am an eyewitness, especially as it relates to serving a long prison term along with three friends who were in attendance that day. To conclude, I reminded my fellow Cubans that, they too were refugees.

The conference was a call to its participants –U.S. and Latin American Professors– to create a bridge between North and South America.

"The book ends here, but the search continues"
Thomas Merton

144

Personal photos

FLORIDA INTERNATIONAL UNIVERSITY
Commencement Ceremony
April 22, 1986

MY GRADUATION
BACHELOR DEGREE IN SCIENCE
APRIL 20, 1986

MY TWO SONS
IGNACION AND DAVID GARCIA

**MY FRIEND JOSE OCTAVIO GUZMAN IN MIAMI, FLORIDA
WITH WHOM I WAS CAPTURED IN CUBA
BY THE STATE SECURITY**

**WITH MY PRISON FRIENDS FROM CUBA, IN MIAMI
NINE TEJADA, PACO ECHEVARRIA, TOMAS FERNANDEZ-TRAVIESO,
ANTONIO COLLADO AND REINALDO MORALES**

147

MY COUSIN EDUARDO CREWS,
MY SONS IGNACIO AND DAVID GARCIA
AND MY NEPHEW LOLO CREWS
KEY BISCAYNE, FL

**LAW SCHOOL GRADUATION
OF MY SON IGNACIO GARCIA**

GRADUATION OF MY SON DAVID GARCIA

**INAUGURATION OF
PRESIDENTE BARACK OBAMA**

IN THE BACKGROUND STATUE OF FELIX VARELA
IN SAINT AUGUSTINE, FLORIDA

WITH MY WIFE, MY SON DAVID AND HIS WIFE MAGALY
IN THE PLACE OF SPANISH LANDING
SAINT AUGUSTINE, FLORIDA

**CLASSMATE FROM BELEN HIGH SCHOOL:
MANUEL HIDALGO AND HIS WIFE**

**WITH MY WIFE AND MY SONS, IGNACIO AND DAVID
TAMPA, FL 2019**

**MY GRANDCHILDREN
JAKE, TYLER, LUCIANNE, MATIAS AND WESLEY**

153

MY SON IGNACIO WITH WIFE KRISTIN

MY SON DAVID WITH WIFE MAGALY

ANTONIO GARCIA-CREWS FAMILY
WIFE, SONS, DAUGTHER-IN-LAWS AND GRANDCHILDREN

CONCLUSION

A lot has changed in this world since June 22, 1939 when I was born in this planet. A few days later, on September 1, Adolph Hitler invaded Poland thus initiating World War II. A few years later, the Allied victory in 1945, the atomic bombs of Hiroshima and Nagasaki, the Cold War, the Cuban Revolution, the October crisis, the end of the Soviet bloc and the terrorist attack to the Twin Towers in September 11, 2001, etc.

In 2014, 35 years after my arrival in the United States, I made the decision to visit my family in Cuba together with my wife and my younger son David. I was able to make a tour of my childhood, youth, and prison as well as. After this trip, I returned four times, one with my older son who wished to meet the relatives left behind. My last visit was in February 2020.

That last visit was very special because I had the opportunity to visit the Sacred Heart Church in *Reina* street. Father Jorge Cela S.J. welcomed me. Father Cela showed me the whole building, including the actual church. He explained the social and communitarian activities they organized in the premises to benefit the poor neighborhood around the church. Many needs are relieved: help with school homework, , classes to victims of domestic abuse, advice to small businesses and cooperative entrepreneurs, space for the local artists to rehearse, and the printing place of *"Vida Cristiana"*, the leaflet distributed to parishioners after the Sunday Masses. All this in response to Jesus' words:

"Go out to the whole world and make disciples, baptizing them in the name of the Father, the Son and the Holy Spirit."
(Mathew 28, par. 19)

I was enthused to meet Father Cela because I had read his homily of July 31, 2019 in *"Vida Cristiana"* which I receive here in Florida. Father Cela echoed Pope Francis' address to the Jesuits. Today, while thinking of the Pope's convocation to celebrate this year the 500th anniversary of the saint's conversion, I copy a section of Fr. Cela's homily on July 31, 2019:

"We are no longer the triumphant church of long ago. We are the martyr church that boldly faced discrimination, persecution and punishment with courage and patience. We are a weakened, aged, and tired church. However, we still have the missionary energy to create new communities that do not stop before a disappointing environment. We keep the capacity to dream a new world with hope, our hands on the plows to build it without looking back; and the sensibility to approach the poor, the prisoner, the sick, the children, the abused women, not allowing the selfishness flowing through our veins to overcome us."

At the end of his homily, Father Cela stressed four preferences:

The first one has to do with a search for meaning one anxiously feels in the face of disappointment. The second, is to walk together with the poor in a mission of reconciliation and justice. The third one is to accompany the young in their search for a future with hope. The fourth, to cooperate in caring for the common home our Father created for us.

I believe Father Cela's statements on that day opened a path for the Church in Cuba and provided a great example for the Church in the United States. Father Cela died of a heart attack shortly after my visit.

To conclude, I wish to thank God for all he has given me and for my willingness to dream new worlds and to plow without looking back.

Patria y Vida / Fatherland and Life

CPSIA information can be obtained
at www.ICGtesting.com
Printed in the USA
BVHW050038220921
617166BV00005B/14